Adult Sibling Loss

Stories, Reflections, and Ripples

Brenda J. Marshall, PhD, CT

Death, Value, and Meaning Series
Series Editor: Darcy L. Harris

Baywood Publishing Company, Inc.
AMITYVILLE, NEW YORK

Baywood Publishing Company, Inc.
26 Austin Avenue
P.O. Box 337
Amityville, NY 11701
(800) 638-7819
E-mail: baywood@baywood.com
Web site: baywood.com

Library of Congress Catalog Number: 2013009039
ISBN 978-0-89503-827-2 (cloth)
ISBN 978-0-89503-828-9 (paper)
ISBN 978-0-89503-830-2 (e-pub)
ISBN 978-0-89503-829-6 (e-pdf)
http://dx.doi.org/10.2190/ASL

Library of Congress Cataloging-in-Publication Data

Marshall, Brenda J., 1963
   Adult sibling loss : stories, reflections, and ripples / Brenda J. Marshall, Ph. D., CT.
      pages cm. -- (Death, value, and meaning series)
   Includes bibliographical references and index.
   ISBN 978-0-89503-827-2 (cloth : alk. paper) -- ISBN 978-0-89503-828-9 (pbk. : alk. paper) -- ISBN 978-0-89503-830-2 (e-pub) -- ISBN 978-0-89503-829-6 (e-pdf) 1. Brothers and sisters. 2. Brothers and sisters--Death. 3. Grief. I. Title.
   BF723.S43M37 2013
   155.9'370855--dc23
                                        2013009039

Dedication

For my parents.

Table of Contents

Foreword

Years ago, a friend of mine's sister died after the diagnosis of a rare form of cancer. We were both in our early twenties, and we had been friends for many years. During the time her sister was receiving treatment, my friend would often miss social functions and informal gatherings of our group of friends so that she could be with her sister in the hospital during her treatments or help with her care at home. She cut back to a part-time course load at University so that she would have the time to be with her sister and to help their parents in the home. When her sister died, my friend was devastated. Her parents were broken-hearted and my friend was inconsolable. Cards and expressions of sympathy began to arrive at their home. All the cards, flowers, and gestures were sent to her parents. At the funeral, people asked her how her mother was "holding up." Her friends were there to support her, of course, but it was highly apparent that her grief was seen by most people as secondary to the grief of her parents. As time went on, there were numerous indications that my friend was expected to assuage the grief of her parents by over-functioning, being the "good daughter," and not making waves. She failed the next year of her University studies. She went through several romantic relationships, always ending them abruptly. She finally decided to move to the other end of the country, and we lost touch after that. I always wondered about her.

Brenda Marshall shared with me about her experience of losing her brother shortly after our first meeting. Much of her experience resonated with that of my friend. Brenda was acutely aware of what it was like to be the invisible griever after the unexpected death of her brother. It was from the death of her brother that she decided to give voice to other bereaved siblings whose grief has been largely unacknowledged or validated.

The narratives in this book describe a range of grief responses after the death of a sibling. Each story provides unique insights into the bond that siblings can share, the depth of the relational history that is shared between them, and the profound absence that can be felt when the presence of someone who has shared your life with you as you both grew up—is now gone.

The death of a sibling is a unique type of loss that has received sparse attention. The relationships we have with our siblings is unlike any other—we share the same parents, have learned many life lessons from them, and there is always the assumption that you will have each other throughout your life. When a sibling dies, basic assumptions about how family life will unfold are shattered. For siblings who live in the home, there is often the ambiguous loss of the parents due to their unavailability emotionally as a result of their grief, which means that surviving siblings have not only lost a brother or sister, but often their parents and their entire family system as they have known it. This loss is significant, and yet it is typically overshadowed by the acknowledgment and accommodations given to the parents.

A myriad number of books are available that explore the impact of the death of a child on parents, the death of a spouse, and a few more on the topic of the death of a parent for both younger and adult children. However, very little has been written on the topic of sibling loss. The death of a sibling can be both a highly profound and a socially disenfranchised experience. It is our hope that this book opens the door for the voices of bereaved siblings to begin to be heard and recognized.

Darcy L. Harris

Acknowledgments

It is fitting that the last page I write for this book, takes me back to the people who were part of its creation. Like the stories contained within these pages, these relationships and experiences are still in motion. There are authors whose work inspired and continue to inspire me. There are teachers who instilled a passion for learning and colleagues who modeled excellence. And there are friends and family who supported me throughout. There are however a group of individuals whom I would like to honor in a special way.

For Rena, Karen, and Catherine, thank you from the bottom of my heart. You entrusted me with your stories and gave me the freedom to share them with others. Your generosity has created openings for so many and I am deeply indebted to each of you. Every presentation and paper I create is informed by what we learned together.

I am also deeply grateful to the countless siblings named and unnamed in these texts, who have reached out to me over the past few years. Your experiences have added to our collective knowledge on this important topic. For Ian, Susan, and Judy, I am especially grateful for your continued support and validation of this work.

Thank-you to Carmen Shields, friend and mentor who first introduced me to narrative ways. You gave me a way to move with this experience. Thank you also to Gary Knowles, Ardra Cole, Solveiga Miezitis, and Gail Lindsay each of whom served on the committee that supported the original work.

Thank you to Darcy L. Harris, Series Editor: *Death, Value, and Meaning,* and visionary. You continue to open new doors and possibilities for me and model excellence and empathy in all you do. You are a true "seer" of all that is possible.

For Susanne, C & J, you are a continuing blessing in my life and as intertwined in these stories as I am.

For my family, thank you for understanding how important this was to me. You quietly applaud everything I do from the sidelines.

And finally, thank you to my husband John Watters who provides the safest harbor one could ever want. Your steadfast support, encouragement, and belief in possibilities brought this text to life.

PART ONE

Introduction

Figure 1. "We Three."
Source: Family Photo, Brenda, 1973.

Mourning . . . is not replacing the dead but making a place for something else to be in relation to the past. . . . We bring the past to the present, we allow ourselves to experience what we have lost, and also what we are—that we are—despite this loss. (Behar, 1996, p. 175)

"How was your Christmas?" my friend asked. "Good," I replied. And I genuinely meant it. Surprising really, given how much a part of Christmas Brent always was. As kids, we used to race down to the tree together on Christmas morning, eager to tear open our gifts. Stockings came last, for they were filled with fruit and socks and things not nearly so fascinating as what was under the tree. As we grew older, I loved picking gifts for him. Hockey equipment, shirts, sweaters, and one year a "fish" tie. Brent had recently begun his first "real" job and now wore suits to work. I remember his quizzical look as he pulled the colorful salmon out of the box. "Ahh . . . it's a fish, Brenda," he said. "Yes, it's the latest trend—you'll see, they will all be wearing them!" I replied. The trend never took off, but Brent made the tie a regular part of his suit rotation. Time passed and holiday time changed. We had families and homes of our own, and getting together at Christmas was one of the few times our family would reunite at one table. I remember our last one, all of us wearing those silly colored paper hats you find in Christmas crackers. Thirty-seven Christmases together, and now our sixth without him.

Brent died from a strep infection[1] on September 16, 2006. He'd been sick with the flu for a few days and then suddenly worsened and was rushed to hospital by ambulance. I remember taking the call at work. "You need to leave now," my husband said. "Brent is in the emergency department in kidney and liver failure." I don't recall much about the drive. We arrived, and were met by Brent's wife who cautioned me about what I was about to see. We took turns sitting by his side that day and night. At first, he was conscious and could speak, barely. An oxygen mask covered his face. Tubes, wires, and machines covered the rest. "I used to have such big breaths," he said to the nurse. "Yes, your lungs are filling with fluid. We're over-hydrating you to get your kidneys going again." He nodded. I gripped his arm. "Ice," he pleaded to his wife. She spooned some into his mouth and then retreated to the corner of the room. I remember her eyes—wide, frightened. The buzzer. "Your mom is here," a nurse

---

[1] The New York State Department of Health provides an excellent overview of Group A strep infections and their potential complications. Brent died from streptococcal toxic shock syndrome (STSS). This is an infection that moves through the body rapidly, causing low blood pressure/shock and injury to organs such as the kidneys, liver, and lungs. Approximately 60 percent of people with STSS die. Retrieved March 3, 2009, from http://www.health.state.ny.us/diseases/communicable/streptococcal/group_a/fact_sheet.htm

called to me. Inwardly I groaned. She came directly from another hospital where she was with my father, just days removed from knee replacement surgery. I tried to prepare her, steadying her as we approached Brent, now lying on a stretcher in the hall as they readied him for another procedure. I remember the way she stroked his hair, and leaned in to whisper to him. His eyes met hers. "Help me, Mom," they seemed to say. My eyes welled. Another buzzer. Another visitor. Only immediate family now. And so it went, rotating throughout the night, Brent worsening as time passed. On life support, he was airlifted to another hospital in a last try to restart his kidneys. I remember the frantic drive across the city, pleading with God to let him survive the flight. He did and we settled in at hospital number two. I paced the hallway counting my steps. Minutes. Hours. I lost track. In the distance another family sat silently, heads bowed. "This is what a hospital is like at 4:00 a.m." I remember thinking. Then, a scream, the physician's words and a nurse making me drink orange juice as I rocked back and forth on the floor. He died less than 24 hours after being admitted to hospital. I stopped breathing. The world went on.

> "We're having a family camping weekend," Mark, our landscaper continued. He'd been at our house for a few days digging out our driveway. "I hope it doesn't rain—will be miserable." "Our family used to camp," I interjected. "It absolutely poured on our last trip. At the time I just wanted to leave. But I look back longingly because a couple of months later, my brother died. And so I think about the trip differently now." With that Mark scooped up his shovel and walked away. Not a word spoken. No eye contact. I'd broken the first taboo: I'd talked about my brother's death.

For the longest time, I'd forget Brent was dead. At first it was every morning. I'd open my eyes and instantly feel uneasy. Something was wrong. And then like a thundering wave, I knew, and a dreadful, sick feeling enveloped my body. How could this be? How could my brother really be dead? Over time, the morning jolt subsided. I'd still get it, but at odd times during the day. I recall walking down the hall of a busy shopping mall and suddenly realizing we'd had our last conversation. Our last one. I began to cry, busy shoppers brushing by, and me, locked in my own misery among the mundane tasks of daily life. These moments of forgetfulness were so painful, almost as though a new layer of myself was learning for the first time what the rest of me knew. In retrospect, I wonder if this was my brain's way of easing me into a new reality. Worden (2009) calls this task one: accepting the reality that your loved one is gone. It went on for a long time.

Brent's death changed everything about my life. The way I related to my family, my spouse, Brent's surviving family, friends, work—everything—shifted and I felt like a stranger. The order, neatness and predictability were gone. Attig (2001) calls it "the loss of assumptive world." Chodron (1997) calls it "groundlessness." Maya Angelou (2006, p. 48) writes that we "see with a hurtful clarity." I thought of all the people I'd known over the years who'd experienced the death of their loved ones. How woefully inadequate my words of sympathy now seemed. Nothing prepared for me for the dreadfulness of life without my baby brother. For a full year I refused to answer the question "how are you?" with anything other than "OK." It was my private rebellion against joy. Everything now was tainted. To experience joy, to laugh, to feel happy seemed impossible and disloyal. If my brother couldn't have his life, then, I would not enjoy mine.

> "Here's a picture of the three of us. That's Brent, with the goatee," I said to my colleague. She paused. "That doesn't look like you." "Well, it's a few years old and I've probably put on some weight." "No. It's not that," she continued. "You look happy here. I've only known you as sad."

I'm not sure when I began to live again. I do know that writing saved me. Within days of Brent's death I began a journal. At first I marked time. "It's been 12 Saturdays" one entry begins. "I called your cell phone today," begins another. I wrote him letters, speaking in real time about my adventures with his two children. There are poems, random thoughts, and always the sign off, "I love you, Eddie"—the special name I had for him. Writing became an anchor and a way of trying to make sense of what happened. Putting words on paper gave me an outlet for my emotions and, later, a purpose to try and move forward. Through writing I began a journey of what I came to call "integration." It was not "healing" but a re-learning of myself. I had to discover who I was now. My journal gave me freedom to call Brent by his name without fear of making others feel uncomfortable. We were still talking, he and I, and that gave me comfort. On paper I discovered just how much a part of my identity he was. Our verbal jousting, the regular phone calls, that feeling of connection, impossible to recreate with another. My brother, my little brother, the first "other" for whom I felt a duty of care and concern. My first experience of empathy. My first big responsibility—the protection and safety of a younger sibling. All of these lessons first learned because I had a little brother.

Hunt writes, "If applied research is to be authentic and relevant, researchers must first accept their own personhood, their co-participation in the human venture they seek to understand" (1992, p. 116). The idea for a research project came gradually. At the time of Brent's death, I was in the midst of doctoral studies. Authenticity in leadership was an area of interest. No more. Brent's death overshadowed all, consuming my thoughts from the moment I awoke until I slept. I lost my ability to feel empathy for anyone other than those who were grieving. Siblings, in particular, held my interest for I'd become acutely aware of how little the world knew, or seemed to care, about sibling loss. Very soon after Brent's death, I realized few viewed me as a griever. I was to be a supporter. Comments and questions from friends and colleagues always centered on Brent's wife and children and our parents. "How are they doing?" "It must be dreadful for them." "Why," I wondered, "am I invisible?" Why were all the bereaved siblings I met similarly isolated?

My research (Marshall, 2009) was a narrative inquiry into the experience of sibling loss. I gathered stories from other grieving siblings, weaving my own story through theirs. When we came together, there was joy. We talked back and forth about our beloved brothers and sisters, and through conversation, introduced them to more people. Like me, they too were frozen out of conversations about their siblings. "She's right here at this table," Rena, one of the participants, said to me at one of our meetings. My research opened new doors, and as opportunities to write and present continued to arise, Brent's presence in my life only increased. Our relationship grew.

"The grave does not obliterate the place of the sibling in the family" (Klass, Silverman, & Nickman, 1996, p. 233). There were and are so many layers of "remaking" since Brent died. I continue to remake myself, my career, my future plans. This book is my latest "remaking" of self. I always envisioned Brent and I would be neighbors in our old age. He'd be my constant, the person who I could always count on. And because he was younger, absolutely, he'd be with me always. My husband lovingly referred to him as my "back-up spouse." I remade a place for myself in his family, becoming actively involved with his children. "Tell me another story about Daddy," is a common request from his kids. I am the repository of a history they will never hear firsthand. Through stories I try to give them an essence of the man they knew so briefly. I love talking about him. They ask me questions, and, through conversation, he comes closer. Remaking my family of origin has been harder. My parents continue to find it difficult to speak of him so mostly we don't. Getting used to leaving him out of family conversations continues to be a struggle.

> "Oh, your job sounds so difficult," my dentist said. "Working with grief—must be so awful." Although my mouth was full of instruments, I managed a garbled, "No, actually it's not. It's joyful."

The distance traveled between September 16, 2006, and now is astounding. To experience a "good" Christmas, to feel joy and enthusiasm and passion for life beyond what I had before, is remarkable. I feel as close to Brent today as I did when he was alive. How is it that a relationship can continue to develop after death? White (1988/1989) calls this "saying hullo again." Yes, I've said hello to Brent again. No longer do I fear that the passage of time will cause memories to fade and his imprint on the world to slip away. He's continuing to reach out and connect with others through my stories. "Your paper about your brother makes me want to write about mine," a stranger recently wrote to me. And while I am thankful that the acute pain of his death has receded, a deep sadness remains. These brief connections across time zones and countries, though, help keep me whole. They reinforce the key message of this text. Our siblings matter.

Pema Chodrin (2010) speaks of "leaning in" toward that which makes us uncomfortable. I'm fortunate that my natural inclination was to go toward my pain, to study it, turn it over, even drown in it. Years ago on a white-water rafting trip in Australia, we had to exit our boat and go over a small waterfall on our own. Even with my lifejacket on, the whirlpool sucked me to the bottom of the river. I could see sunlight but could not move toward it. Just when I thought my lungs would explode, I shot to the surface. The power of nature, my inability to fight a current I could not see, humbled me. And then, 20-some years later, the universe humbled me again. Nature put me on this path, and trying not to follow it is harder than going with it. I am leaning in.

"I write because I want to find something out. I write in order to learn something that I did not know before I wrote it" (Richardson, 2000, p. 924). I also write because I want to continue our sibling conversations. Every time I present or share excerpts from this text, another bereaved sibling connects and shares his or her story. Ripples. It reinforces how much our siblings matter and how important it is to keep talking about them. Their stories open doors for others to speak and, in turn, new connections are formed. This book is part of continuing those conversations.

Building off the original research and resulting dissertation (Marshall, 2009), I will include new insights and developments. In the next chapter, I'll share what I've learned of sibling relationships from the literature. Together we'll explore what makes these relationships unique and how they shape our lives. In the final chapter of this section, I'll discuss narrative, my chosen research method and methodology, and the value of stories. This way of looking and thinking about life has been enormously helpful to me. It also sets the stage for the stories you'll read in part two. There you will meet Rena, Karen, and Catherine, and learn of their deceased siblings and how their relationships evolved over time. And while other family members play a role in their stories, it is the experiences of these three women that we focus on. In part three, I'll discuss the themes that emerged both from the original work and which continue to be validated in my ongoing conversations with bereaved siblings. We'll also examine some of the challenges bereaved siblings face and how that mirrors many of the themes expressed by children who lose their siblings. And finally, we'll close with personal letters from Rena, Karen, and Catherine updating readers on where they are today.

REFERENCES

Angelou, M. (2006). *Celebrations*. New York, NY: Random House.

Attig, T. (2001). Relearning the world: Making and finding meanings. In R. Neimeyer (Ed.), *Meaning reconstruction and the experience of loss* (pp. 33–54). Washington, DC: American Psychological Association.

Behar, R. (1996). *The vulnerable observer: Anthropology that breaks your heart*. Boston, MA: Beacon Press.

Chodron, P. (1997). *When things fall apart*. Boston, MA: Shambhala.

Hunt, D. E. (1992). *The renewal of personal energy*. Toronto, ON: OISE Press.

Klass, D., Silverman, P. R., & Nickman, S. L. (1996). Bereaved siblings. In D. Klass, P. R. Silverman, & S. L. Nickman (Eds.), *Continuing bonds: New understandings of grief* (pp. 233–234). Philadelphia, PA: Taylor & Francis.

Marshall, B. (2009). *Silent grief: Narratives of bereaved adult siblings* (Doctoral dissertation, University of Toronto, Toronto). Available from University of Toronto Research Repository. (http://hdl.handle.net/1807/19153)

Richardson, L. (2000). Writing: A method of inquiry. In N. K. Denzin & Y. Lincoln (Eds.), *Handbook of qualitative research* (2nd ed.). Thousand Oaks, CA: Sage.

White, M. (1988/1989). Saying hullo again: The incorporation of the lost relationship in the resolution of grief. *Dulwich Centre Newsletter,* Summer.

Worden, J. W. (2009). *Grief counseling and grief therapy.* New York, NY: Springer.

Siblings Matter

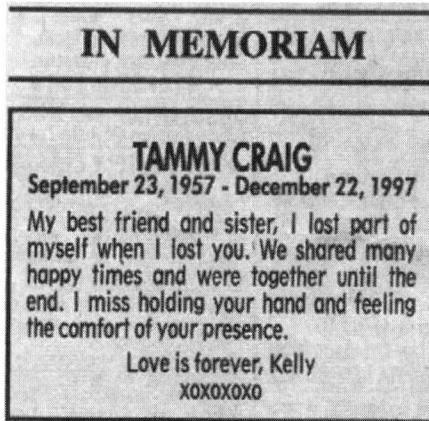

Figure 2. **Source**: *Toronto Star,* December 22, 2008, B5.

I never used to read obituaries. Occasionally, if someone I knew died, I'd look for the notice and then quickly move onto another section of the newspaper. But after Brent died, reading them became a focus. I'd scan the pages looking for others who died young. There was something about knowing I wasn't the only one mourning a young person that made me feel just a little less alone. I'd read the words carefully, reflecting on the life lived as presented in this small square of text. When siblings were mentioned, instantly I'd feel a jolt, and tears would flow as I reflected on what might lie ahead for them. And while siblings had a prominent place in this forum, they were mentioned by name, I knew that soon after the funeral, their loss would fade into the background as other family members became the focus.

In the weeks following Brent's death I approached the local chapter of a community-based bereavement support organization seeking assistance. I was surprised to learn there were groups for widows, friends, parents, and children who had lost parents—and yet none for siblings. They had a good-sized library of resource material available for loan and not a single article or book specific to sibling loss. Even the counselor I spoke with was surprised she had nothing to offer me. Eventually I did find a few books, *Sibling Grief* (Gill White, 2006), *Surviving the Death of a Sibling* (Wray, 2003), and *Letters to Sara: The Agony of Adult Sibling Loss* (McCurry, 2001); however, it was only due to my own drive to find a resource. This experience, although difficult, was a turning point for me. It marked the beginning of my research—my need to understand why my loss didn't merit the same attention as others. And, I wanted to change that perception.

Soon after this experience, I noticed the memoriam section of the newspaper for the first time. Different from obituaries, these were announcements placed in memory of those who died years before. And here, I saw a trend. Virtually every time I reviewed this section, there was at least one placed for a beloved brother or sister. Some died 40 years prior. Imagine, for 40 years a bereaved sibling took the time to either select a verse or write one, and place it in this public space. I began saving them. I have more than 80, carefully

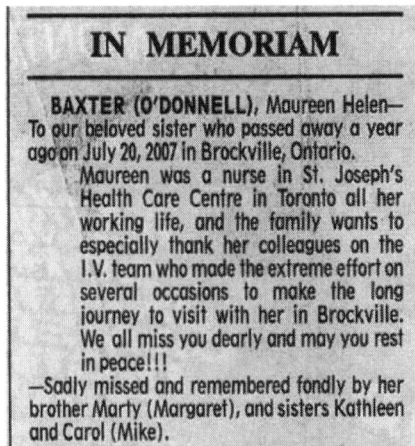

IN MEMORIAM

BAXTER (O'DONNELL), Maureen Helen—
To our beloved sister who passed away a year ago on July 20, 2007 in Brockville, Ontario.
Maureen was a nurse in St. Joseph's Health Care Centre in Toronto all her working life, and the family wants to especially thank her colleagues on the I.V. team who made the extreme effort on several occasions to make the long journey to visit with her in Brockville. We all miss you dearly and may you rest in peace!!!
—Sadly missed and remembered fondly by her brother Marty (Margaret), and sisters Kathleen and Carol (Mike).

Figure 3. **Source**: *Toronto Star*, July 19, 2008, CL 11.

catalogued and stored—my way of honoring another's sibling. Some commemorate birthdays now being celebrated in absentia. Others detail changes in the family, as though the author is sending their sibling a letter. Ones placed years and years post death were a double-edged sword for me. In the early days, they validated that it was okay for me to feel as dreadful as I did. At the same time, they were a frightening look at what lay ahead. It didn't matter how many years passed, these individuals continued to mourn their deceased brother or sister. I would still miss my brother.

In our society we expect and acknowledge that bereaved parents will long for their deceased child forever. The death of a child is often referred to as the worst loss (Rosof, 1994), and bereaved parents are expected to live scrambled lives forever as they continually renegotiate what the loss means. But what of the siblings? Long after parents die, siblings remain the sole torch carrier for a life that many will forget. They tend to the gravesite after parents die, hold stories for their deceased sibling's children, and carry the knowledge of how the family once was. Unlike a surviving spouse who may find love and partnership with someone new, siblings do not find a "new" brother or sister. And, just as bereaved parents miss their child forever, siblings do too.

Sibling loss is often referred to as disenfranchised loss (Doka, 2002; Wray, 2003; Zampitella, 2006). It is not typically recognized as being as significant as the loss felt by other family members. Among adults, concern is most often directed toward the surviving spouse and children, and then for the deceased's parents. I saw this firsthand and heard it in the voices and stories of the participants in this study. While surviving siblings often played prominent roles in the days leading up to the death, attending medical appointments, sitting vigil at the hospital, and acting as the key point person for the family, after the funeral they took on the role of "grief supporters" versus grievers. "How are your parents?" is likely the most common question bereaved adult siblings get. When I suggested this to an audience recently, there were heads nodding and even laughter.

Our society, through many prominent institutions, promotes the idea that siblings are not primary grievers. Certainly my earlier example of my local bereavement support organization sends a message. Their website lists groups for everyone except siblings, which by omission, contributes to the view that we don't need one. Even within organizations like the military and police force, both of whom have well-established policies and procedures for dealing with the death of members, typically siblings are not included in their post-loss bereavement support programs for family members. At a recent presentation I gave (Marshall, 2011), several members of a military family support service were present and sitting together at one table. At the conclusion of my presentation, I asked for volunteers to share any insights they'd gained. One member from the group said, "We just realized we don't include siblings. We want to change that." Dr. Heidi Horsley,[1] an expert on sibling loss, ran bereaved sibling workshops for 9/11 sibling survivors of firefighters. She heard over and over that they did not feel their loss was validated or acknowledged. They did not receive the services that were allotted to the widows and children of the deceased firefighters nor did they receive the public recognition that was given to other family members. It was not until the fourth year post-9/11, that siblings were invited to read the names of their brothers and sisters at the public memorial (H. Horsley, personal communication, May 6, 2009).

Within hospice settings, there is a similar theme. Adult children of the patient and/or the patient's spouse are typically assigned the decision-making role as it relates to the care of their dying loved one. And after the death, they are automatically included in bereavement programs if they choose to attend. Siblings are not. And yet, I've heard many stories from palliative care professionals about the key role siblings play in supporting their dying brother or sister during the illness. Susan, a bereaved sibling herself, and spiritual counselor at a hospice in the United States, shared a story about one of her elderly patients. The patient's sister, elderly herself, called her sister every day for weeks. And when the patient was very near her death, it was her sister who spoke with her in her last hours of life, sharing stories of their lives together. Susan made special arrangements so that the surviving sister could access the bereavement support that all the other family members were automatically entitled to receive.

The relationship people share with their siblings is potentially *the* longest one they will ever have (Cicirelli, 1982; Gill White, 2006). Longer than parents, spouses, or friends, our relationship with our siblings has the potential to be lifelong. Siblings know each other in

---

[1] Dr. Heidi Horsley is Cofounder of the Open to Hope Foundation, an online bereavement support resource. The foundation was created in memory of her brother. Retrieved May 11, 2009, from http://opentohope.com/

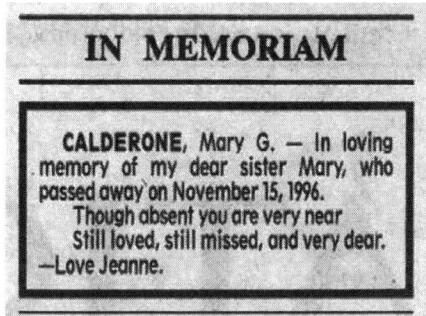

IN MEMORIAM

CALDERONE, Mary G. — In loving memory of my dear sister Mary, who passed away on November 15, 1996.
Though absent you are very near
Still loved, still missed, and very dear.
—Love Jeanne.

Figure 4. **Source**: *Toronto Star*, November 15, 2008, CL 15.

ways friends and other blood relatives do not. We have shared bedrooms, bathrooms, holidays, school days, family milestones, meals, and a way of growing up that people outside the family cannot ever fully understand. The bond is intense, complicated, sometimes difficult, often wonderful, and absolutely irreplaceable. And unlike selecting a friend, spouse, or life partner, a sibling simply arrives and there is no choice but to be in a relationship; you are connected for life. There are shared jokes and memories that are so numerous they form an underpinning of familiarity that can never be achieved with anyone else.

My older brother and I always called Brent "Eddie." His middle name was Edward, and this "pet" name was initially meant to tease. It started when we were younger and over the years it just stuck. Everyone around us knew who "Eddie" was—but we were the only ones who used it. It was our private sibling connection. Even in adulthood I thought of Brent as my baby brother—someone I needed to look out for and take care of. I used to love introducing this big hulking guy that way at parties. People would smile. We played prominent roles for one another in key milestones of our lives. He was the master of ceremonies at my wedding and I spoke at his. I am the godparent to his daughter. He was and still is the named executor of my will. I spent virtually every Christmas, New Year's Eve, Thanksgiving, and Easter with Brent for 38 years. "If not for death, they [siblings] would be with us longer than anyone else on earth" (Vaught Godfrey, 2006, p. 7). Who wouldn't miss someone who had been such an integral part of their lives for so long?

MAZZARA, David (Harley, Cowboy)
— In memory of our loving brother.
Dave had many names throughout
his life. When we were just kids his
name was Santa Claus.
We respected his ideas and
leadership. Dave also had a keen wit
and a cheerful sense of humour.
We are sure his co-worker pals miss
his friendly character.
This would have been his 63rd
birthday today and he left us too
soon.
—Gary, Alfie and Louise.

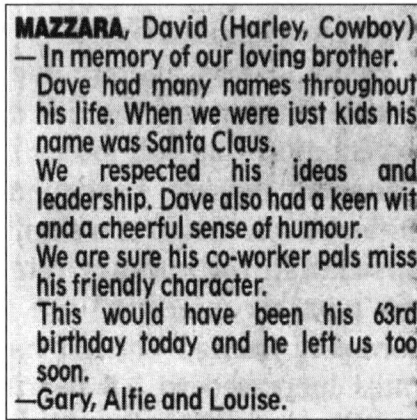

Figure 5. **Source:** *Toronto Star,* January 22, 2009, B8.

Connidis (1992) studied 60 sibling dyads aged 25 to 89 to explore
the effect of life transitions on what she called the adult sibling tie.
For the majority of those in her study she found that siblings
remained an important and valued connection throughout life. And,
although some participants noted there were times when they were
in less frequent contact with their brother or sister, for the most
part the closeness of the sibling tie was something that participants
felt could be rekindled or mobilized when needed. "Siblings remain
lifelong parts of most adults' social networks" (White, 2001, p. 566).
Studies have shown that the average adult has contact with a sibling
once or twice a month for 60 or 70 years after leaving home (White
& Riedmann, 1992). And while other relationships (spouse, children)
may be more central for most adults, the sibling relationship is
incredibly durable over time.

These studies pre-date the use of social media as a form of communication, when staying in touch was done through phone calls,
letters, and visits. I'm certain if repeated today, the reported
frequency of contact would be even higher. However, I have also
learned that the level of closeness felt is sometimes unrelated to
frequency of contact.

In workshops, I often ask participants to draw three concentric
circles. Then I ask them to consider all the people who are part of
their lives (living or dead), and place their names in the circle that
best represents "how close" they feel to that individual. The inner

circle represents those with whom they feel most connected. The vast majority place the names of at least one of their siblings in the inner circle, regardless of how often they speak to one another. This exercise often leads to a discussion about the relationship, how distance and time apart do not impact how they feel about their sibling. The room is instantly animated as people eagerly exchange stories about their brothers and sisters. Many speak of siblings who live continents away and whom they now rarely see. "But I still feel totally connected" is a common refrain. No matter the group, this activity consistently brings about smiles, laughter, and high energy within the room. This fits with White's (2001) discussion of the standard kinship model that considers family ties as a set of nested circles. Siblings often begin in the inner circle, shift to the other outer circles as individuals begin their own families, and then come back in as both age. Siblings, she observes, are "permanent but flexible members of our social networks, whose roles in our networks are renegotiated in light of changing circumstances and competing obligations" (p. 557).

All three participants in this study spoke with their siblings regularly, some even daily. They enjoyed outings together, lunches, shopping, weekends away, and just time talking on the phone. Their children played together, they supported one another through difficult times, celebrated mutual successes, and were a constant emotional presence. Goetting (1986, p. 704) writes, "perhaps the most important task of siblingship throughout the life cycle is that of providing companionship, friendship, comfort, and affection." And as we will discuss, the loss of a future together is a significant part of their grieving experiences.

Gill White (2006) created a website called the Sibling Connection[2], dedicated to bereaved siblings. Her own sister died in childhood, and she was haunted by the experience throughout her adult life. Initially the website was for adults whose siblings died in childhood. Later she expanded it to include a section for those whose siblings died in adulthood, and now much of her counseling practice is focused on bereaved siblings. In her work, she's found some common grief reactions. Many siblings find they must seek a new identity, separate from the one developed with their sibling. As there has been much research to suggest that birth order plays a role in how

---

[2] Retrieved March 3, 2009, from http://www.counselingstlouis.net/page3.html

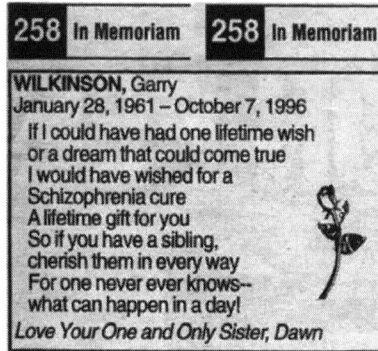

Figure 6. **Source:** *The Aurora Era-Banner,* October 7, 2008, p. 19.

individuals relate to the world, suddenly losing someone from that order creates a crisis. The family structure is significantly altered by the absence of a key member, and everyone must redefine their relationships and roles. Others discover they need to work through the trauma associated with the death of their sibling—especially in cases where death was sudden and unexpected. I too recall struggling with the difficult sights and sounds of Brent's last 24 hours. I was the only one from my family present when he died—my brother and mother were awaiting updates from another location and my father was also hospitalized. For months after, the image of how he looked just before he died was a constant in my day. I couldn't erase it. I saw his face, features distorted and discolored and heard the sounds of machines performing every function for him. I recalled the feeling of his arm when I reached for it. It was so cold, icy— I automatically recoiled. I remember thinking, "Is he dead?" These thoughts were intrusive and I wanted to say them aloud, to share them with another family member. I wanted someone to know, understand, and acknowledge how dreadful it was for me to see my beloved brother go through this. And yet, I knew to share these images would cause them too much pain. I kept to them to myself, recording some of the more difficult memories in a journal.

"Everyone deals with grief differently." This is a common refrain I have heard since Brent died. I see it in my family and also in the families of others I have come to know since his death. Within my family, most typically I am the one who initiates stories or mentions his name. I want to bring him into the conversation, to say "remember when Brent did..." and share a laugh. Others, though, are quiet, reserved, and more private about their feelings. As Catherine, one of the participants in this study, so aptly described "you get to learn what you do and don't say" quickly. Each of the participants in this project echoed a similar pattern within their own families. They all struggled to reform and establish new ways of communicating with one another and most often, conversations about their sibling were rare. "The grave does not obliterate the place of the sibling in the family" (Klass, Silverman, & Nickman, 1996, p. 233) and yet, their death often obliterates the opportunity to share stories about them, a key theme I will address in part three.

A few years back I did a quick review of top-rated television shows. I counted more than 10 where the relationship between siblings was central to the plot line. Many of them are now discontinued but they ran for years. *Brothers and Sisters* (Olin, Berlanti, Osusu-Breen, & Schapker, 2007), was a drama about the intricacies of adult sibling relationships. *Two and a Half Men* (Loree & Aronshohn, 2003), currently running with a revised storyline, was originally based on the story of two brothers attempting to share a home after one of them is divorced and forced to move in with the other. Similarly in *Hope and Faith* (Johnson, Levisetti, & Bruce, 2003), a younger sister moves in with her elder sister and family after losing her career. Their obvious personality differences form the basis for many comedic moments in the show. The themes though represent what the research tells us about the value of our siblings. We turn to them in good times and bad times, and just expect that they will always be there. Even when they are not part of the central story in our lives, their presence is felt. They are vital to our sense of self and connect us across so many different spheres of our lives.

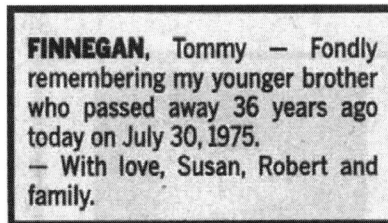

FINNEGAN, Tommy — Fondly remembering my younger brother who passed away 36 years ago today on July 30, 1975.
— With love, Susan, Robert and family.

Figure 7. **Source:** *Toronto Star,* July 30, 2011, GT 10.

In Memoriam

Christopher Edward Earl
7/11/68-1/28/07

Last year, the day after my brother died, I wrote an e-mail to my friends and colleagues in which I said God must need him more than we do. I said I wouldn't hold this loss against God and that I'd try to accept it graciously. I cried as I was writing it, just as I am now. I believe I've been true to my commitment to accept it graciously and I think that's how Chris would have wanted it. I was reminded recently of another commitment I made a number of years ago, one in which Chris supported me, to "cease fighting anything or anyone". I've very recently come to a place of true acceptance in this and the realization of it left me feeling somehow taller, spiritually lifted, and I think that's also how Chris would have wanted it. But I still miss my brother.
Tom Earl

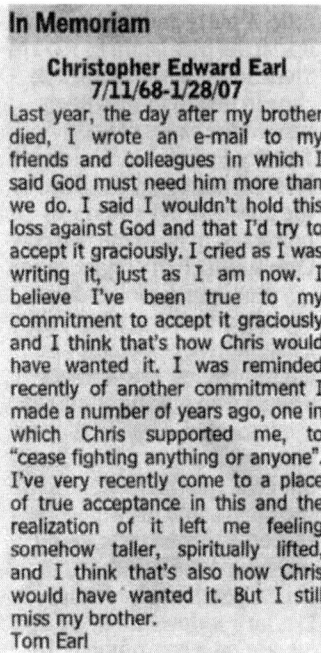

Figure 8. **Source**: *The Globe and Mail,* January 28, 2008, p. 40.

I remember a gentleman seeking me out after a presentation (Marshall, 2008). Although he was not a bereaved sibling he faced challenges with his two adult sisters from whom he had grown apart. "Your presentation made me think about how much I'd miss them if they were gone," he said. "I'm going to try and work things out." As I think is the case for most people, the relationship they share with their siblings is one that is taken for granted. It is unfortunately only in its absence when the depth of it is most acutely felt. Even those who describe difficult and problematic sibling relationships in life still feel deep pain after their death (Berman, 2009). Our connection is unconditional.

REFERENCES

Berman, C. (2009). *When a brother or sister dies: Looking back, moving forward.* Westport, CT: Praeger.

Cicirelli, V. (1982). Sibling influence throughout the lifespan. In M. E. Lamb & B. Sutton-Smith (Eds.), *Sibling relationships: Their nature and significance across the lifespan* (pp. 267–284). Hillsdale, NJ: Lawrence Erlbaum Associates.

Connidis, I. A. (1992). Life transitions and the adult sibling tie: A qualitative study. *Journal of Marriage and the Family, 54*(4), 972–982.

Doka, K. (2002). Introduction. In K. Doka (Ed.), *Disenfranchised grief* (pp. 5–21). Champaign, IL: Research Press.

Gill White, P. (2006). *Sibling grief: Healing after the death of a sister or a brother.* New York, NY: iUniverse, Inc.

Goetting, A. (1986). The developmental tasks of siblingship over the life cycle. *Journal of Marriage and the Family, 48*(4), 703–714.

Johnson, J., Levisetti, E., & Bruce, J. (Writer). (2003). *Hope and Faith* [Television series]. New York, NY: American Broadcasting Company.

Klass, D. (1996). The deceased child in the psychic and social worlds of bereaved parents during the resolution of grief. In D. Klass, P. R. Silverman, & S. L. Nickman (Eds.), *Continuing bonds: New understandings of grief* (pp. 199–216). Philadelphia, PA: Taylor & Francis.

Loree, C., & Aronshohn, L. (Writer). (2003). *Two and a half men* [Television series]. Malibu, CA: Columbia Broadcasting Service.

Marshall, B. J. (2008, April). *Adult sibling loss: Disenfranchised grief and the sibling connection.* Paper presented at annual conference of the Association for Death Education and Counselling, Montreal, QC.

Marshall, B. J. (2011). *Adult sibling loss. Disenfranchised grief and the sibling connection.* Paper presented at the Canadian Grief and Bereavement Conference, Toronto, ON.

McCurry, A. (2001). *Letters to Sara: The agony of adult sibling loss.* New York, NY: 1st Books.

Olin, K., Berlanti, G., Osusu-Breen, M., & Schapker, A. (Writer). (2007). *Brothers and sisters* [Television series]. Los Angeles, CA: ABC Studios.

Rosof, B. D. (1994). *The worst loss: How families heal from the death of a child.* New York, NY: Owl Books.

Vaught Godfrey, R. (2006). Losing a sibling in adulthood. *The Forum, 32*(1), 6–7.

White, L. (2001). Sibling relationships over the life course: A panel analysis. *Journal of Marriage and the Family, 63*(2), 555–568.

White, L., & Riedmann, A. (1992, September). Ties among adult siblings. *Social Forces, 71*, 85–102.

Wray, T. J. (2003). *Surviving the death of a sibling: Living through grief when an adult brother or sister dies.* New York, NY: Three Rivers Press.

Zampitella, C. (2006). Using nature-based rituals as an intervention for adult sibling survivors. *The Forum, 32*(1), 9–15.

Narrative

"Oh my God, I can't tell this anymore," I suddenly thought. The group was waiting for the end of my story—waiting to hear me say, "and my brother Brent. . . ." I stopped. I felt that familiar sick feeling, the one I get when I've forgotten and then remembered again. "Who was he now? My brother who died, my 'late brother' or was he still just 'Brent?'" I was too far in so I replaced him in the story with my older brother's name. I felt disjointed after. The story wasn't true anymore and it wasn't fun to tell. (Brenda, personal story, 2008)

As the idea for a research project formed, I knew for certain it would be a narrative inquiry. Narrative as a research method assumes stories are always in motion and allows for the intimate interplay of researcher with participants. I would be free to build relationships and connections without feeling pressured to bracket myself out of the story. My involvement and participation in the phenomenon I was to study was a given; I would be living, telling, reliving, and retelling my own story (Connelly & Clandinin, 1990) as the research progressed. And, just as telling/writing stories about my brother helped me, I believed other bereaved siblings might also find comfort in doing so. Narrative allowed for this kind of flow, to story, and restory; it was "as much a philosophy as a method" (Gilbert, 2002, p. 237).

Within the research community, quantitative methods of inquiry are more commonly understood and accepted as "research." There is a search for evidence or the "truth," and the researcher's voice or point of view is mostly absent from the study. Narrative, on the other hand, places the researcher/author into the story, and assumes there is no absolute truth to be found. As a research method, it often brings people together. "When we share stories from our lives, we begin to open ourselves to others and perhaps nowhere are others more willing to come close enough to hear them as when they are being told a story" (Shabatay, 1991, p. 150). The unit of measurement is the story and researchers work closely with participants as partners in creating how those stories are told. Readers are invited to reflect on how the stories they read resonate in their own lives and to come to their own conclusions about meaning. I'd used this methodology for many years and willingly accepted my role as a co-creator of the research that underlies this book. Indeed, I felt my place as a bereaved sibling gave me a unique advantage in this process.

I worked in-depth with three women; Rena, Karen, and Catherine. All of them were bereaved siblings, between the ages of 35 and 55. Their siblings (Cookie, Brian, & James, respectively) died within the preceding 12 years. I defined "siblings" as someone with whom the participant shared both biological parents and lived within the same home while growing up. My choice to work within these parameters was deliberate. First, from reading and speaking with other bereaved siblings I observed that the most acute time of transition came within the first few years following their sibling's death (Gill White, 2006). Changes in how they processed that loss continued for years after; however, the immediate years following the death appeared to be the most profound. Second, I believed that part of feeling disenfranchised came from societal/cultural expectations around the importance or perceived lack of importance of the sibling connection into adulthood. Once individuals moved away from home and began their own families, society generally views the family of origin as less important to their well-being. By selecting participants who were in their mid-thirties to early forties at the time of their sibling's death, I assumed each person would be well onto their own lives apart from their family of origin. As well, the death of a sibling within this age range would still be viewed as "out of pattern." Losing a sibling at age 80 represented a "normal" lifespan. Losing one at age 40 was not. And last, I anticipated our shared age demographic would invite more connection. As Edwards (1993, p. 185) notes, "researchers bring their own life experiences to their research, and they structure what the research is about."

We met individually multiple times over several months, completing more than 35 hours of taped interviews. Because of our shared loss we had conversations about our siblings in a way that others unfamiliar with the experience could not. It was not simply me asking prescriptive questions and awaiting answers. We talked back and forth, in conversation, more like friends than interviewer and interviewee (Cole & Knowles, 2001). In line with what Johnson

(2001) called in-depth interviews, my experience and stories were obvious to the participants and often we discussed the similarities and differences. My goal was to create an authentic connection, to let "the principles of reflexivity, relationality, mutuality, care, sensitivity, and respect guide the development of questions for conversation" (Cole & Knowles, 2001, p. 73). My position as an insider (Farnsworth, 1996) helped me understand and relate to the intimate stories that I heard. Interjecting stories of my own life helped to unfold new ones and prompt deeper discussions. "One way of knowing about others' intimate experiences is to reflect on our own" (Ellis, 1993, p. 725).

At our first meeting, we discussed and agreed upon the topics that would guide our time together. We revisited this list regularly, using it more like a prompt than a contract. Our conversations wove back and forth, from their lives to my life, and across a multitude of timeframes. It was not a linear process but more like a meandering walk through the past, present, and future as we talked about the roles siblings played in each of our lives before and after their deaths. I tape recorded our interviews and had them transcribed. I shared the transcripts with each woman and invited them to change/edit as they wished. Interestingly, none chose to do so—save for updating a few factual items. Each of our subsequent meetings began with a quick review of our last meeting and then a discussion about emerging themes from the transcripts. Sharing the transcripts and reviewing themes together was another opportunity for each woman to "sift out, from their wealth of experience, stories to tell us" (Cole & Knowles, 2001, p. 119). Their narratives were and are central to all that flowed from it, and I wanted the final text to represent their stories well.

> A qualitative design is emergent: One does not know . . . what to ask, or where to look next without analyzing data as they are collected. Hunches, working hypotheses, and educated guesses direct the investigator's attention to certain data and then to refining and/or verifying one's hunches. (Merriam, 1988, p. 125)

While interviews were my primary method of gathering stories, I also invited the women to share meaningful photographs and artefacts as part of our conversations. The use of artefacts and photographs within a narrative inquiry framework is not uncommon (Bach, 2007; Connelly & Clandinin, 2006). The photographs prompted new stories that added to the richness of our conversations. It was as though the images took each backward in time, where they recaptured the moment and feelings associated with that event (Pinnegar, 2007). Rena's photo of Mother's Day, the last one shared with her sister, was especially important to her. Karen liked the photograph of Brian holding her daughter. For her it symbolized how much her brother cared for her. She also laughed at one, recalling that her brother had just had his wisdom teeth removed a few hours before. Catherine liked the one of James, standing atop a mountain appearing happy and content in the outdoors he loved so much. As Harrison (2002) notes, "there are stories about photographs, and there are stories that lie behind them and between them" (p. 105).

With Karen, her "memory box" of mementoes of her brother was often at the table with us for each interview. Without prompting, she naturally pulled items and photographs from it as we spoke, giving me the background, often smiling at the memory. At our last meeting we walked into her garage to find Brian's drywall stilts. They were buried deep among other stored items. Finding them prompted a story about his life as a tradesman and his experiences in western Canada. Rena enjoyed searching for and then selecting the items to bring, noting that it was "many years since I've looked at these things." For Catherine, our walk together through her home to look at James's possessions was a reminder for her of how present he continued to be in her life. She was genuinely surprised at the number of items she had. I noted how prominently displayed they were—in some cases, the focal point in the room.

Within narrative, it is not unusual for researchers to move back and forth from data gathering to data analysis simultaneously. My data analyses began during the interview conversations when we discussed emerging themes from the prior meeting. That discussion became a part of the transcript, creating a written record of our evolving conversations. I also kept a reflective journal to record my own emotional reactions to the work and information gathered. I photographed all the artefacts, anticipating they would be helpful as I moved deeper into the analysis phase of the project. I also wanted to leave open the possibility to include visual representations as part of future presentations—which proved to be a good choice. I have now used them in several presentations, and their impact is striking as they convey visually the depth of the connection in a different way than words do (Marshall, 2009). As Weber (2008) notes, photographs can make stories more memorable. "Images elicit emotional as well as intellectual responses and have overtones that stay with us" (p. 45). And by design, I begin each woman's narrative with a photograph of their sibling and end with a photograph of the items they chose to keep after their sibling's death.

Once I completed all the interviews I worked separately with each person's transcripts, reading and re-reading them while listening to the recordings. I also looked at the images of their treasured artifacts as I listened to the tapes again. I highlighted quotes that resonated with me from each interview transcript and then looked for themes across the selected quotes. Once I "named" those themes, they became the bedrock for the various sections of each person's narrative, letting the simple vignettes act as anchors to the broader story of connection. I wrote many drafts before landing on a version that I was comfortable sharing. I sent each woman's narrative to them for review and then met individually to experience their reactions. All of them liked how our stories were woven together and none requested any significant changes. Each one invested much of herself in this work; I was so grateful. For me, the creation of the individual narratives formed the cornerstone of my writing and, once I had their approvals, other chapters evolved around their three stories.

In the next round of analysis I looked for themes across the three narratives, trying to draw a larger picture into focus. I also returned to the research, professional and trade literature, reviewing articles I had read before and finding new ones to go along with knowledge I was uncovering. At this stage, I asked each participant to select a few photographs of their siblings that they would be comfortable sharing with an audience. Through photographs, each participant and her brother or sister became real people. As Weber (2008, p. 45) notes, "images can enhance empathic understanding," which I believed would assist in educating others about this loss. In keeping with narrative methodology, as my knowledge of this topic has continued to evolve, I continue to add and refine presentations and papers.

The notion of informed consent (Cole & Knowles, 2001), more typically associated with preserving anonymity and protecting participants from harm, seemed more complex when I moved from field texts to written texts and later presentations. Because each participant chose to use her own name and the name of her deceased sibling, I felt great weight of responsibility as a researcher to "do no harm." And what of stories about someone who was now deceased? I was writing about someone who could not offer his or her thoughts or opinions, and I wanted to honor their memory. I reflected deeply on this notion. Later when the work was completed and I began creating conference presentations, again I was mindful of my responsibilities. What might be comfortable in a written format might not be so in a public presentation. Would they want their photographs shared this way? Even though each signed consent documents that detailed all the ways I envisioned the work might be used, I still chose and choose to keep them informed about my plans. And, in every case I am prepared to remove any references or photographs that they no longer want in the public eye. As noted by Connelly and Clandinin (2006), narrative researchers have a higher duty of care as they create their work. What constitutes respect and compassion in the minds of this researcher/participant pair is the nature of the implicit contract between them" (Josselson, 2007, p. 539). And from my perspective, the contract needs to be reconsidered with every new element. Even in finalizing the writing for this book, I opted to share chapters where I felt their presence was especially visible. And in order to preserve anonymity for family members around each, some details, names, and ages, were changed for this text.

My overarching goal with the research was to explore the experience of adult sibling loss through the eyes of four bereaved siblings. There are many texts that deal with the experiences of bereaved parents but few where the sibling story is *the* story. And while each sibling's experience unfolded (and continues to unfold) as part of a family, parents included, I wanted their individual stories to be central. As part of that, I also wanted to understand what a "sibling bond" looked like for each individual. Each of the participants described feeling very closely connected to their deceased sibling. I listened for stories of how that connection presented itself, when it first formed, and how the relationships changed as they aged. I also wanted to know if and how they kept their deceased sibling present in their lives after death. Silverman and Klass (1996) were the first to suggest that continuing bonds with the deceased was a normal part of the grief experience. Rather than trying to leave the relationship behind, it continued in a new form. Silverman and Klass's work normalized what had previously been considered an unhealthy response to grief. It was not necessary to break ties with the deceased in order to move forward. In fact, part of moving forward in grief came from renegotiating this relationship. Last, I wanted to understand if they too experienced silencing as I had.

Tuchman (cited in Richardson, 2000, p. 942) writes, "the writer's object is—or should be—to hold the reader's attention. . . . I want the reader to turn the page and keep on turning to the end." My goal with the narratives, in particular, was to first honor each participant and their sibling and then, hopefully, to make a connection with you, the reader. The stories you are about to read have become the central focus for many of the presentations I give on this topic. Rena, Karen, and Catherine love to hear how their stories resonate and, when possible, have attended. As Rena said once, "I feel proud when I see my sister's picture on the screen." All of them are excited that our work together is now in book form and are eager to see their siblings' stories continue. To Rena, Karen, and Catherine, I now turn.

REFERENCES

Bach, H. (2007). Composing a visual narrative inquiry. In D. J. Clandinin (Ed.), *Handbook of narrative inquiry* (pp. 280–307). Thousand Oaks, CA: Sage.

Cole, A., & Knowles, G. (2001). *Lives in context. The art of life history research*. Walnut Creek, CA: Altamira Press.

Connelly, F. M., & Clandinin, D. J. (1990). Stories of experience and narrative inquiry. *Educational Researcher, 19*(5), 2–14.

Connelly, F. M., & Clandinin, D. J. (2006). Narrative inquiry. In J. L. Green, G. Camilli, & P. Elmore, B. (Eds.), *Handbook of complementary methods in education research* (pp. 477–487). Washington, DC: American Educational Research Association.

Edwards, R. (1993). An education in interviewing: Placing the researcher and the research. In C. M. Renzetti & R. M. Lee (Eds.), *Researching sensitive topics* (pp. 181–195). Thousand Oaks, CA: Sage.

Ellis, C. (1993). There are survivors. Telling a story of sudden death. *The Sociological Quarterly, 34*(4), 711–730.

Farnsworth, E. B. (1996). Reflexivity and qualitative family research: Insider's perspectives in bereaving the loss of a child. In J. F. Gilgun & M. B. Sussman (Eds.), *The methods and methodologies of qualitative family research* (pp. 399–415). Binghamton, NY: Haworth Press.

Gilbert, K. (2002). Taking a narrative approach to grief research: Finding meaning in stories. *Death Studies, 26*, 223–239.

Gill White, P. (2006). *Sibling grief: Healing after the death of a sister or brother*. New York, NY: iUniverse, Inc.

Harrison, B. (2002). Photographic visions and narrative inquiry. *Narrative Inquiry, 12*(1), 87–111.

Johnson, J. A. (2001). In-depth qualitative interviewing. In J. F. Gubrium & J. A. Holstein (Eds.), *Handbook of interview research: Context and methods* (pp. 103–119). Thousand Oaks, CA: Sage.

Josselson, R. (2007). The ethical attitude in narrative research. In D. J. Clandinin (Ed.), *Handbook of narrative inquiry* (pp. 537–566). Thousand Oaks, CA: Sage.

Marshall, B. J. (2009, April). *Silent grief: A narrative inquiry into the meaning making processes of bereaved adult siblings.* Paper presented at annual conference of the Association for Death Education and Counseling, Dallas, TX.

Merriam, S. B. (1988). *Case study research in education: A qualitative approach.* San Francisco, CA: Jossey-Bass.

Pinnegar, S., & Daynes, J. G. (2007). Locating narrative inquiry historically: Thematics in the turn to narrative. In D. J. Clandinin (Ed.), *Handbook of narrative inquiry* (pp. 3–34). Thousand Oaks, CA: Sage.

Richardson, L. (2000). Writing: A method of inquiry. In N. K. Denzin & Y. Lincoln (Eds.), *Handbook of qualitative research* (2nd ed.). Thousand Oaks, CA: Sage.

Shabatay, V. (1991). The stranger's story: Who calls and who answers. In C. Witherell & N. Noddings (Eds.), *Stories lives tell: Narrative and dialogue in education* (pp. 135–155). New York, NY: Teachers College Press.

Silverman, P. R., & Klass, D. (1996). Introduction: What's the problem? In D. Klass, P. R. Silverman, & S. L. Nickman (Eds.), *Continuing bonds: New understandings of grief* (pp. 3–27). Philadelphia, PA: Taylor & Francis.

Weber, S. (2008). Visual images in research. In A. Cole & J. G. Knowles (Eds.), *Handbook of the arts in qualitative research* (pp. 41–53). Thousand Oaks, CA: Sage.

PART TWO

Rena and Cookie

Figure 9. "Sisters."
Source: Family Photo, Rena, 1993.

COOKIE
(April 3, 1944—August 8, 1997)

I was sitting with her when the porter came to take her up to intensive care. "They're taking you now." She had the oxygen mask on her face but she lifted it and said, "Are you coming with me?" Those were the last words she ever spoke to me. (Rena, June 11, 2008)

I met Rena in Montreal at the Association for Death Education and Counseling (ADEC)[1] 2008 conference. It was my first academic presentation (Marshall, 2008) and the first time I formally spoke about sibling loss. I had one hour to speak. A quick poll at the beginning of my session confirmed what I expected would be true. In addition to being grief professionals, most of the attendees were themselves also bereaved adult siblings.

I built audience participation sections into my session; however, I was unprepared for the number of people who wanted to talk, some tearfully, as they spoke about the loss of their sibling. One woman asked if she could read a poem written in memory of her sister. Another told the story of witnessing two elderly sisters lying side by side in a hospital room, one near death, holding hands across the aisle. Later in the day I saw that same woman again in the lobby of the hotel. She told me about her brother who died when she was 12 years old. She was now in her 70s and her eyes welled as she recalled watching her mother open the telegram delivered to their door advising the family that he died in battle. These experiences further reinforced for me that there was a place for my research, that it would matter to people beyond myself. I closed the session with a PowerPoint presentation set to music that flashed memorials written for deceased siblings that I had collected from the newspaper. When the music ended, the room was silent. A woman sitting in the front stood and thanked me for my presentation and then turned to the audience and suggested "everyone ought to hug." It was so moving to be among people sharing similar losses.

Rena was a member of the audience. She waited to speak with me afterwards and gave me her telephone number letting me know

[1] ADEC is an interdisciplinary organization in the field of dying, death, and bereavement. It has nearly 2,000 members from a wide array of fields. Additional information may be found on its website. Retrieved March 3, 2009, from http://www.adec.org/About_ADEC.htm

Figure 10. "Mother's Day."
Source: Family Photo, Rena, 1997.

(This photo was taken on Mother's Day 1997. Cookie died later that summer. Rena carries this picture with her on all her travels.)

that she was from Toronto. I didn't realize it at the time, but she also was a bereaved sibling and wanted to learn more about my planned research. I assumed she was working in the field and was looking for someone to connect with who lived locally. She told me later that there was something that had compelled her to attend my workshop even though, for professional reasons, there was another session that was more relevant to her work. This one, she thought, would be for her.

We met a few weeks later in a local coffee shop. Rena quickly recounted the story of her sister's death, showing me some pictures as she did so. One, in particular, was well worn from being carried around many years, carefully packed to go with her on all of her trips. At this meeting, I also learned Rena was soon to be ordained as a rabbi and that her Rabbinic thesis was in the area of bereavement. She wanted to be one of my participants. At that time my research plan was already established and I wondered if I could accommodate another participant. I also wondered how I might be able to engage someone in conversations who very clearly was already well entrenched in the field. I thought about it for a few days, made some changes to my plans, and then let her know I was pleased to have her join. I had found a third participant.

GETTING ACQUAINTED

When she was in grade 6 or 7, my mom took me to watch her in a school play. I was very young—we had an almost 10-year age difference. I remember Cookie walked out on the stage to do her part and I yelled, "There's Cookie!" We always laughed about that later. (Rena, June 11, 2008)

Rena chose to meet me either at the university or at my home. Although I was willing to travel to meet with her, I sensed she wanted to keep our work somewhat removed from her immediate family. Unlike Karen, whom I knew from childhood, and Catherine, whom I had connected with through business, Rena and I were strangers to one another when we began. We were separated in age and religion, and our family situations were very different. She had been married twice as long as I had, and her children were grown adults and well into living independently.

Where we did connect was with the loss of our siblings and the place and role they had played in our respective families. Rena was the youngest of three children. There was her brother, Shane[2], who was 13 years her senior, Cookie, 10 years older, and, then, herself. Rena described her sister as the "glue" of the family, the one that got along best with everyone and who was a favorite of her parents. Like Brent, Cookie was the hub around which everyone revolved. She brought people together and made them feel good about themselves. We laughed about the collective memories of our siblings who were gifted with more patience than either of us. Both, it seemed, were the ones best suited to handle the idiosyncrasies of aging parents. It sounded as if Cookie and Brent were of a similar temperament, easy-going, kind, and caring. We even joked that "perhaps they now knew each other in heaven," so similar were their roles in our families.

[2] Pseudonym for Rena's older brother.

Rena and I also shared an interest in the academic side of grief and bereavement. She had practical experience in leading grief groups and conducted funerals as one of her professional roles. I enjoyed exchanging ideas with someone who was passionate about the field. She was modest about her accomplishments and took our work together very seriously. We got to know each other through our stories, and I looked forward to our regular meetings. While our losses were different, there was a commonality in the way we each chose to respond to that loss that was comforting.

MY BIG SISTER

And I remember when she got her first job. She always used to buy me things from Laura Secord. For Halloween there would be a chocolate pumpkin or a witch, all these different things that they sell. She was always thinking of me that way. (Rena, June 11, 2008)

Cookie was a wonderful presence in Rena's life from the day she was born. "She was always very loving; she was like a little Mommy" (Rena, June 11, 2008). Through the eyes of a younger sister, I could hear Rena's deep admiration for her older sister. Cookie made Rena feel safe in the world. "She was my big sister and so that meant that there was a lot of protection there. A lot of protection and comfort and companionship and fun" (Rena, June 11, 2008). As kids she remembered Cookie as the one who took the most interest in her, almost like a "really fun" parental figure. When her sister married and had children, Rena became the babysitter. And later when Cookie moved from their home in Montreal, to Toronto, Rena soon followed and they formed their own tight family unit. Their relationship evolved over time; Cookie was her mentor, confidante, friend, and partner in so much of her life. They spoke on the phone daily and spent hours together doing, what Rena later called, "ordinary things." She smiled at the memory of picking up the phone and hearing her sister say simply "me." It was their private sibling connection.

Brent and I had that same link. We talked almost every day, never usually about anything of high importance, just a comforting presence in the middle of the day. His number was programmed into my cell phone for ease of dialing in the car. We both had long commutes to and from work, and we often passed the time chatting

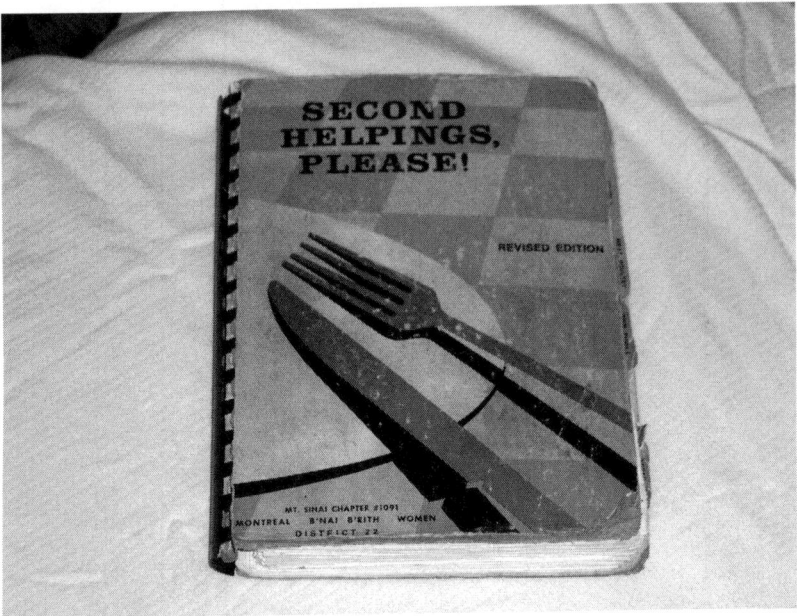

Figure 11. "Favorite Cookbook."
Source: B. Marshall, 2009.

(Cookie gave Rena this cookbook, and the two of them used
it often when preparing meals together.)

while driving. We called them our "traffic calls." For the first few weeks after he died, I called his cell phone just to hear his voice. A couple of times I even left a message. It was unbelievable that he was physically gone; yet, through technology he seemed alive. As long as I could hear his voice, I felt I still had a link. And then one day, when I called, the number was disconnected.

Cookie died from non-Hodgkin's lymphoma in 1997. Nearly 11 years had passed when Rena and I began our interviews. I was not quite two years removed from Brent's death and for the other participants, seven and eight years, respectively. Many of Rena's memories focused on the last four years of her sister's life when she battled cancer. It was hard to select happy stories as many of the more recent ones detailed the progression of her sister's illness. Rena was a nurse in a prior career and so her recounting of her sister's illness was very detailed. She remembered each medical event very clearly and painstakingly walked me through all the stages, attaching dates and times to each. I learned, from talking to her, cancer was only the underlying issue. As the disease progressed, and her sister's immune system weakened, she became a host for many other painful disorders, some life threatening on their own. She went from medical crisis to crisis, always just barely hanging on.

> At that point, I was working at Women's College and she was at Toronto General, so every day on my lunch break, I would go to see her. On the weekends, same thing. I never missed a day. All the staff knew me there. I remember one day, she had such bad diarrhea, like she was a mess. And I said, "Okay, I'm going to get you into the bathtub." I was wearing a suit. She said, "You can't do this." I said, "I'm going to get you in the bathtub and we'll call for the nurse." I couldn't go out and come back in and leave her like that. And she always remembered that I got her into the bath; I cleaned her up. (Rena, July 2, 2008)

Later when I re-read Rena's transcripts I tried to look beyond the descriptions of the disease and medical appointments and find the overarching story told. I saw this time period as representing a fairly dramatic shift in their relationship. With the lead role in Cookie's care, Rena moved from being the adoring younger sister to the more protective older sister, committed to helping Cookie make it through each crisis. She was there for all the physician appointments and kept her extended family appraised of Cookie's ever-changing condition. Her sister's illness, and her role as caregiver, became the central focus of her life during that time for she was with her sister every day. We did not talk much about her own children or other relationships or how she managed her own household. All the conversations revolved around what happened with Cookie.

Rena's devotion reminded me of my grandmother and her sister. They lived together for more than 30 years. My grandmother moved in with her sister when my grandfather died. She was the younger of the two and from the outside it appeared that she always deferred to her older sister. My great aunt seemed to be the "boss" of the house and made all the decisions, from where furniture could be positioned to what they were going to eat each day. But when my great aunt had a stroke and needed extra care it was my grandmother who stepped in and ensured she could return to their home. She bathed her, prepared meals, and looked after her pills and without

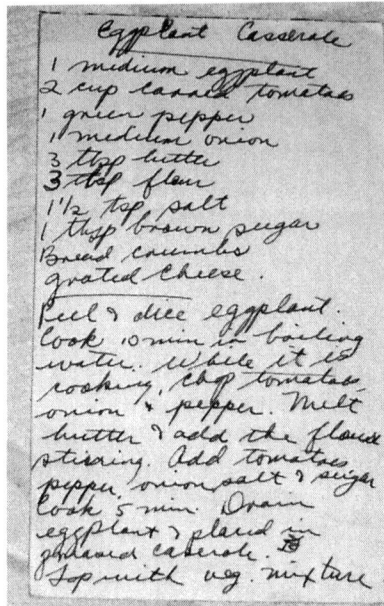

Figure 12. "Recipe."
Source: B. Marshall, 2009.

(This was a favorite recipe of Cookie's and Rena's.)

her sister, my aunt surely would have lived in a long-term care facility. They lived well into their 90s and, when my great aunt died, my grandmother died soon after.

Rena's care helped keep Cookie alive. Her daily visits, liaisons with the medical team, and constant attention was a lifeline for her sister. She played a role in every decision surrounding her sister's care. Cookie was the main focus in Rena's life throughout her illness.

THE VOID

It's all about the void that's left. Suddenly there's a gap, and that person isn't there. And it's not a matter of someone not living in the house . . . but she had such a significant part of my life and she wasn't there anymore. And no one to answer the phone at the other end of the line to come in and say, "Hi, guess what I did at work today?" Or for her to call . . . (Rena, June 11, 2008)

As I discovered with each of the participants, there was a deep and ongoing sadness about losing a sibling. Rena was devastated by Cookie's absence. "So even though I've been married to my husband for now 33 years, I didn't grow up with him. We didn't have the same family of origin and the same way of looking at things that our parents had taught us," she said to me. "I would be terrible at making a decision, so she was always the person I would bounce things off of and there wasn't that partner anymore" (Rena, June 11, 2008). The place that Cookie held in Rena's life was irreplaceable. She left a "gigantic hole," the same description I heard from each participant. Rena likened it to a scar or disability that remained after a serious surgery. You simply had to find a way to work around it. Rena's comment about the special nature of the connection she had with her sister, and how it differed from the one she had with her husband, would soon be echoed word for word by Karen. For both of them, the connections felt to their siblings were in many ways deeper than what they had with their spouses. Links as blood relatives from the same family superseded everything else.

From our very first conversation I knew that Cookie was the family member with whom Rena felt most connected. Although Cookie did not attend university she applauded Rena's academic accomplishments and made her feel special for everything she did. "She went to school vicariously through me . . . she always thought, 'good for you, if that's what you think you want to do and you can do it, then go for it'" (Rena, July 2, 2008). The two of them were alike in their approach to life, and it was as though they created a smaller sub-family unit within their birth family that was a mutually supportive environment. I could tell how much Rena loved her sister. And later, when she showed me some of the greeting cards her sister had sent her, I was struck by the deeply emotional words Cookie wrote to her. It really seemed like a very, very special relationship.

> I had once worked out that my parents would die and given the fact that women outlive men, I would probably outlive my husband. And she would probably outlive her husband and the two of us would be together. I mean, we'd have our children— but the two of us, we'd be together. Through all those other losses, we would have each other. (Rena, July 2, 2008)

One of the hardest hurdles for Rena to overcome was accepting the loss of a future with her sister. She felt sad seeing other sisters together out shopping or having coffee, feeling like she had been denied what would have been such a lovely, long-term connection. She assumed Cookie would always be part of her life. I smiled at her story for I had a similar unspoken assumption about Brent. As my husband John was older than I, I also assumed that a time might come when I would be on my own. I took a little comfort knowing Brent, as my younger brother, would always be with me. I could buy a home near him and share in the joy of his children, being their special "aunt Brenda." Because of the kind of person he was, and his dedication to family, I knew he would include me in his life. I would never be alone.

"It just wasn't supposed to work that way. We were . . . supposed to grow old together" (Rena, July 2, 2008). Rena said this many, many times in our conversations. As I discovered with the other participants, there was an unspoken expectation that our siblings would be with us our entire lives. We could picture and accept our parent's eventual death and even that our spouses might predecease us. None of us ever imagined that our sibling would die. It just was not supposed to be.

FAMILY RELATIONSHIPS

> I remember going with her to that first day. The strangest thing is I even remember exactly what I wore to the appointment. The nurse was great and explained everything to her. I was there for support. She was pretty sick the next day. The nausea started very quickly, and those six months were rough. She had about six chemo sessions. I went to nearly every one of them. (Rena, July 2, 2008)

Rena's lead role continued after her sister's death. She stayed with Cookie's body until it was taken by the funeral home, as is the custom in Judaism. She helped organize the funeral and delivered the eulogy. And later, when Cookie's husband needed help with packing up her clothing and other belongings from their home, Rena was the one who did it. She recalled how after the room was packed and all of Cookie's things moved out, she wept, saying to her brother-in-law, "now this room is empty of her." Rena was available for every difficult task while her sister was alive and then, even, after her death. She took her role and responsibility as a sister very seriously, almost as if by doing these things, she was extending their bond beyond life.

Taking on this role was not without personal cost for Rena. I had heard others express a feeling of being entitled to feel sadder about their sibling's death than other family members because they had endured the most or had the closest relationship. I recalled one of the audience members from the presentation (Marshall, 2008) at ADEC sobbing as she described how her remaining siblings distanced themselves after the youngest sister's death, the silence continuing to this day, years later. Although nearly 11 years had passed since Cookie's death, Rena still felt deeply saddened, even angry, at her brother for not coming through for her sister in the way she expected. "Nobody grieves the same way and nobody grieves the same individual. I grieve the sister who was my older sister. He grieves his younger sister" (Rena, July 22, 2008). Her brother never made it to Toronto to say "good-bye" to his sister, not truly believing that she was as near death as Rena described to him. I also sensed Rena felt abandoned with her grief within her own family. They never acknowledged the dreadful nature of the experience of caring for her dying sister. Rena was with Cookie through every step of her illness and, after the funeral, the rest of her family stayed with her only briefly and then returned to their homes in Montreal. Rena was left to sort through her grief on her own.

> It can't ever be. That jigsaw puzzle can't ever be the same picture, because a piece is missing. And I think the piece that's missing becomes the central piece. Like, wherever the main focus of the picture is, it might be in the top corner, I don't know, but I think that is the piece that's missing. There's something huge in that one little piece that's lost. (Rena, June 11, 2008)

"My parents did not talk a lot about her. My mother, not at all. My father, a little bit. But my parents really were never the same" (Rena, July 22, 2008). Rena's parents were in their 80s when her sister died. Elderly, they struggled to cope afterward and both died within a few years of their daughter's death. During that time, though, Rena and her brother took on more responsibilities for their parents. Things that previously were easy for them to do became difficult and they required more care. They also lost their zest for living. "Before when I would go with Cookie to visit there was always a great joy . . . everyone would come over . . . my father loved that. And after she died . . . they were very happy when I would go . . . but there wasn't that joy. . . . The spark was gone" (Rena, July 22, 2008).

Figure 13. "El Penon."
Source: B. Marshall, 2009.

(Cookie brought this tin of coffee back for Rena from one of her trips.
Rena kept the tin long after the original coffee was used up,
and it has sat on her kitchen counter for many years.)

As time passed, Rena noticed tension in her interactions with her sister's adult children. For the first several years they continued to get together for special religious holidays. And then, very unexpectedly, Cookie's husband died and it became harder to maintain the same connection. Rena also went away to school for several years, which created a physical distance from her sister's children. She recalled that she and her niece differed in how they wanted to remember Cookie. "There were times when I wanted to talk about Cookie and she would say, 'I don't want to talk about it'" (Rena, June 11, 2008). Rena wanted to bring her sister into the conversation and found it painful to leave her out.

Similarly, in my family there are differences in the ways we choose to remember Brent. I like to see his face in the photographs I have placed throughout our home. It keeps his image fresh in my mind and reminds me of the many activities we shared together. My parents choose to keep photographs in more private locations. In a room in their basement is a beautiful wall of memories. Brent's lacrosse and hockey sticks are carefully placed on the wall among photos and other remembrances of his achievements. Their choice to keep this wall private is in many ways symbolic of their grief, which they also choose to keep to themselves. Until recently, our conversations unfolded in a similar manner. Sharing memories of Brent most often were met with silence, with the conversation quickly coming to a close and changing direction. It is only within this past year (2012) that I've noticed a shift.

Rena described her family after Cookie's death as a "matrix that got rearranged and never worked quite so well again." Without Cookie in it, the relationships were different and strained. She did not talk much about how her own immediate family had changed other than to say her children knew it was okay to talk about Aunt Cookie and that, after she died, Rena changed as a parent. She found it hard to hear her daughters argue. Having had such a peaceful and loving relationship with her own sister, she wanted her own children to feel the same about one another. She wanted them to understand how lucky they were to have one another and to recognize the specialness of the relationship. Every one of the participants expressed a similar sentiment. After having and then losing such a close relationship, they wanted their children to understand and value what it meant to have a close sibling.

MAKING MEANING

> I love traveling. I always used to bring something home for her when I would go on a trip but then after she died . . . I couldn't. The only thing I could ever bring for her is a stone to put on her monument. So that's what I do. I'm always looking for a stone to bring back for her. And then I go visit her and put it on her monument. There are lots of stones there. (Rena, August 11, 2008)

With Rena, my conversations about meaning making were much more direct than with the other participants. She was already familiar with it as a concept in grief work, understanding the importance many researchers placed on it as a means of recovery. She was easily able to reflect on her life and select the aspects she felt were reflective of her own journey. At times she shared a story and then realized she had not thought about it in a very long time. And often that made her smile. As I looked back on the transcripts of our conversations, I realized we talked about meaning making in one form or another almost every time we got together. It was ingrained in her life.

With the other participants, their siblings died suddenly and unexpectedly under what could only be described as unusual conditions. Their time of death was difficult to pinpoint, and both deaths were traumatic. For them, part of their meaning making came from trying to understand the actual circumstances surrounding their sibling's death. How they died and what lead up to their death were critical questions. Rena was an active participant in her sister's care during her struggle with cancer and was present at her death. For her, then, this part of the experience seemed like it was already settled. "In a weird way I couldn't believe that she died. On the other hand, it was a relief that she, finally, was out of pain" (Rena, June 11, 2008). In her eulogy for Cookie, Rena spoke of moving from praying for her sister to survive to praying for God to take her and relieve her pain. She saw it as one of the last loving acts to do for Cookie, knowing that when Cookie's pain ended, hers would begin. "Things happen. I don't believe that there's some larger force that decides. . . . It happened. She got cancer" (Rena, August 11, 2008). As I reflected on the conversations we had over the summer, I realized that I never heard Rena question why her sister got cancer in the first place. She certainly felt it was unfair that she lost her sister, but she was not looking for an answer as to why. I wondered if she already made sense of that years earlier when Cookie was first diagnosed. Perhaps if we had met then, the story would have been different. Now, though, it was clear that she accepted her sister's explanation. "It was the luck of the draw."

In the immediate days following Cookie's death, Rena and her family sat Shiva.[3] This is the first of several structured stages of mourning provided for in Judaism, all designed to gently support and guide mourners through the initial coming to terms with their loved ones' death. I was struck by the deep thought and care behind determining these stages, for they invited community support,

[3] A stage of mourning in the Jewish faith. Retrieved March 3, 2009, from http://www.aish.com/literacy/lifecycle/The_Stages_of_Jewish_Mourning.asp

something many find helpful in the grieving process. Every morning for 30 days Rena went to the synagogue and recited the Mourner's Kaddish[4] in memory and honor of her sister. Spoken in community with other grievers, Rena described this as a "lovely prayer, uplifting and positive." It is tradition to recite it every day for one year for a parent and 30 days for a sibling, a spouse, or a child and, in busy and frenetic lives, is a huge commitment. Rena honored this tradition as a further act of love for her sister and at the end of the 30 days gave a tzedakah (a donation) to a charity in memory of her sister. These rituals were important for Rena and helped to support her during the early days after her sister's death. "And that certainly was very important for me and very helpful. . . . Other people at the synagogue knew that I had lost my sister and so there was a lot of enfranchisement there" (Rena, August 11, 2008). Rena continues to honor Cookie every year. She lights a Yahrzeit candle in her home at sundown on the eve of the anniversary of her death and the next morning attends synagogue to once again recite the Mourner's Kaddish in honor and love for her sister.

Coming from a Protestant Christian background, I was unfamiliar with these formal Jewish ceremonies. There was no equivalent in my religion. After Brent's funeral there were no formal religious guideposts to help us along or bring us together. We had to create our own and that was where the differences in how we each dealt with our grief began to show. I invited everyone to our house for dinner on what would have been Brent's 39th birthday. It had only been six months since his death, and I didn't want the day to pass without honoring him in some way. In retrospect, I recognize I was placing my own needs above others, who likely felt pressured to attend whether they wished to or not. I did not realize this at the time. I made a short speech and my sister-in-law read some poetry. It was very emotional. I saw how difficult it was for my parents and, at that moment, I knew I would not hold such an event on his birthday again. As Rena described the formalized symbolism present in Judaism, I could not help but long for something similar in my own life. Somehow I felt that our family would have an easier time coming together and sharing our grief if we had a similar roadmap.

[4] A Hebrew prayer. Retrieved March 3, 2009, from http://www.aish.com/literacy/lifecycle/The_Stages_of_Jewish_Mourning.asp

It was several years after Cookie's death and I came home to find a phone message for me from Canadian Blood Services. It was too late to call them back and so I spent the whole night imagining why they would be calling. I couldn't sleep. I had provided a blood sample for Cookie's bone marrow transplant a few years before. I hadn't been a match for her, but suddenly I was so excited that maybe I was a match for someone else. Maybe this will be a legacy for Cookie. Maybe it's a child, or someone about to get married, I thought. I could hardly wait to call them the next day. I ended up matching on the first six markers but not for the second round of testing. So, in the end it didn't work out, but for that short period of time, there was a lot of meaning there. (Rena, July 2, 2008)

Rena described the initial years after Cookie's passing as an active search for meaning. She wanted to find a way to make her sister's death count for something, describing herself as always "doing" things. She volunteered with local charities and got more involved with her synagogue. "I was always needing to do something conscious. . . . I think I always felt that if I didn't do something tangible, then I wasn't really doing something in terms of meaning making" (Rena, August 11, 2008). And, then, she made the ultimate shift by deciding in her late forties to make a huge career change and attend Rabbinical school. This was a five-year commitment that saw her leaving home to study full time in Israel and the United States. "I knew when I entered Rabbinical school that in four years, when I have to do a thesis, I have no idea what it will be but I know it will be in the pastoral area. That I knew for certain" (Rena, August 11, 2008). Although Rena acknowledged that she was not certain this last decision was a direct result of her sister's death, she did feel that it certainly had influenced her choice and that likely her sister was "guiding her along this road."

I related very strongly to Rena's need to "do something." Shortly after Brent died I applied to be a Big Sister[5] and signed up with Bereaved Families of Ontario to train as a grief group facilitator. I also took unpaid days away from work to visit and play with Brent's children, feeling like it was the least I could do for his family.

[5] This not-for-profit organization matches adult volunteers with children in the community who have been identified as needing additional support. Retrieved March 3, 2009, from http://www.bbbsy.ca/en/Home/AboutUs/default.aspx

I needed to actively seek out ways to make his loss matter. Although I knew there was nothing I could do that would in any way make up for his death, I felt a deep sense of responsibility to try and contribute to the world more fully than I had before. It was also during this time that I decided to change my research focus to adult sibling loss, and I quickly began connecting with researchers in the field of thanatology. It was through those connections that I found myself submitting an abstract and subsequently presenting at the conference where I met Rena. These were all externally obvious signs of meaning making. And in perhaps one of the more dramatic shifts, like Rena, I made a fairly significant career change when I resigned from my job as a management consultant so that I could focus my energy on finishing my research.

Rena also changed as a person. Cookie was always very patient with others and after she died, Rena found she also had more patience with others, especially her parents. She was also more sensitive to people who were grieving and more willing to "go out on a limb" for those faced with tragedy. "I will call that person and I'll go approach the individual, when it would be a whole lot easier not to" (Rena, August 11, 2008). Since Brent's death I am also much more comfortable talking to people about their grief. Whereas before I might have avoided the topic now I do not hesitate to ask people how they are feeling. I am no longer afraid to open that conversation; I know I can listen with care. I liked Rena's new philosophy. "I don't want people to feel . . . that they're in a society in which everybody won't talk about it" (Rena, August 11, 2008).

> And it's almost like she's faded into the background. And even though I have internalized her and I can recognize the connection that we had, she's just not there. I can't reach her anymore. That's probably a healthy thing but to have had something so precious and to have lost it. . . . Sometimes I wonder if I even had a sister. Was that real? Did we really do all those things? Even though she's not completely gone, I know that a part of her is with me spiritually but tangibly she's not. (Rena, July 22, 2008)

As we were nearing the end of our interviews, Rena told me about her plans for the upcoming fall. She was starting another year-long course, this one at a hospital to focus on pastoral care. She was to be the religious person on-call to help people deal with

Figure 14. "Thank-you."
Source: B. Marshall, 2009.

(The name on the notepaper is "Arlene." This is Cookie's given name
although Rena always called her Cookie. Inside was a very
touching thank-you note to Rena for all the love and care
she gave her sister during her illness.)

the last moments of a loved one's life. I thought about the strength
and compassion required for that kind of role. It also took me back
to Brent's last night when we were informed of his death and then,
essentially, left alone in a sterile waiting room trying to absorb
what we had just heard. I rocked back and forth, covering my head
with my arms. I had to remind myself to breathe. Rena would be
the person walking into that kind of situation, trying to offer comfort
to deeply wounded people. "Have I found a meaning for her death?
No. Have I tried to learn things from it? Yes. Have I been successful
at that? Well, not all the time" (Rena, August 11, 2008). Rena smiled
as she said this.

> The most I've talked about losing my sister has been in these
> sessions. I never get to talk to anyone about her . . . really to any
> great extent. Unless I meet someone for the first time and it
> comes up and you know, people will say, "Oh, what did she
> die of?" It's mostly the clinical questions. But to talk like this,
> about . . . ordinary things. (Rena, August 26, 2008)

I was pleased when Rena shared this thought with me. I understood what she meant for I too had enjoyed the freedom of talking
about Brent without the "swoop backwards," as Karen would later
describe it, that I typically got when I mentioned him. When I met
with Rena, we talked and laughed about our siblings without either
of us feeling like we were crossing into forbidden territory.

Even though Rena was the first person I interviewed, I wrote her
narrative last. I started and stopped many times, struggling to find
a flow and capture the essence of our conversations. Part of my
struggle came because I knew how much this meant to her. "I feel
like I'm doing something very important, on many levels" (Rena,
August 11, 2008) she said to me more than once. She was the first
of the three participants to use the word "legacy" to describe what
we were creating. It was a legacy for her sister. I felt the weight of
this responsibility. Cookie was such a large part of Rena's world,
and I wondered how I could find words to describe the depth of such
a special relationship.

> And this . . . these were her earrings, I remember I was with her.
> She bought a suit. A yellow suit and she bought these earrings
> to wear with it and she never liked them because they're clips
> and they hurt her. So she said, "Do you want them?" I said,
> "Okay." I never wore them either. I don't really like them, but . . .
> (Rena, August 26, 2008)

For our last meeting I invited Rena to bring some items that
reminded her of Cookie. I was interested to see the kinds of things
she kept, anticipating that each would prompt a story. There were
earrings which, as she held them, evoked a memory of when they
were purchased. There was an old El Penon coffee tin that had sat
on her counter for many years. There were cookbooks, well worn
and used, which reminded her of all the special meals they made
together. There were a couple of very special greeting cards. In one,
Cookie had written a short poem. "Sisters, sisters, laughing, loving,
sharing, togetherness. In good times and bad times, what is so dear
as sisters like you and me . . . " (Rena, August 26, 2008). I asked Rena

if she thought her sister had composed it herself. "Yes," she replied. "She was always doing things like that." Rena seemed to enjoy showing me each item and talking about why she had it. There was a story for each and, as we talked, she recalled other stories. It had been a long time since she had looked at any of these things, and it made her feel happy. "It's kind of strange. It's almost like going to the cemetery. . . . I don't need to go as often as I used to go" (Rena, August 26, 2008).

I met with Rena to go over this chapter. I wanted her to feel comfortable with a first draft, to feel that it reflected the relationship she shared with Cookie. "I feel like I have come full circle," she said to me. "It's been such a positive experience." When I started my research I was not certain what I would hear from people about meaning making or even if they equated the changes in their lives with that term. I expected that I would need to ask a lot of questions to uncover these shifts, however subtle, in order to understand the larger story that that played across them. With Rena, her awareness of her own process made that easier. She was able to articulate how the changes made in her life were connected with her sister. However, moving to a new level of integration of Cookie into her life was unexpected. There was something in the process of sharing, recording, reviewing, and ultimately creating a narrative that helped her see and feel things that were new. Our work together created another story and avenue for meaning making that she now applied in a new way.

REFERENCES

Marshall, B. J. (2008, April). *Adult sibling loss: Disenfranchised grief and the sibling connection.* Paper presented at annual conference of the Association for Death Education and Counselling, Montreal, QC.Marshall, B. (2009).

Marshall, B. (2009). *Silent grief: Narratives of bereaved adult siblings* (Doctoral dissertation, University of Toronto, Toronto). Available from University of Toronto Research Repository. (http://hdl.handle.net/1807/19153)

Karen and Brian

Figure 15. "Teenagers."
Source: Family Photo, Karen, late 1970s.

(Brian just had his wisdom teeth removed the day before this was taken.
Karen and Brian are leaning against the tailgate of his truck.)

BRIAN
(December 13, 1960—September 19, 2001)

> I came out to the parking lot after work, and Ev was waiting
> for me. That's weird, I thought. "There has been a fire at your
> brother's house and he's missing," he quickly said. Oh, he prob-
> ably slept over at one of his buddy's houses. He'll turn up soon
> I thought. Even after they identified human remains, I still
> didn't believe it was Brian. (Karen, June 11, 2008)

I've known Karen since I was 11 years old. She was one of the first
people I met when my family moved to Agincourt, a small suburb in
what is now the city of Toronto. Karen was a part of my social circle
through high school and into my early twenties. The first one of
our group to marry and have children, she experienced everything
"adult" before the rest of us. I remember her as a happy and helpful
friend, who was always willing to lend a hand to anyone in need.

Figure 16. "Uncle Brian."
Source: Family Photo, Karen, late 1980s.

(In this picture, Brian is holding Karen's oldest daughter. Karen has special
attachment to it because even though Brian had a baby of his own at the
time, he still wanted to hold her daughter. "Because she was important
to me, she was important to him" [Karen, February, 2009].)

She also seemed to know from an early age the importance of being inclusive, making time for the underdogs—the kids in our class who seemed different from the others. Never one to make fun of or tease others, my memory of Karen was of a very gentle person who stayed out of all the "drama" of teenage years. She was a wonderful part of the fabric of my early life.

We lost touch in our mid-twenties and did not reconnect again until our late thirties. By then she had weathered many difficult times. She was just finishing the challenging "teen years" with her two girls—one of whom was already nearly finished with university and the other just getting ready to attend. Her husband, a man I had known since their very first date, had battled and survived a near-death bout with cancer. Her father, now stricken with multiple sclerosis, was very ill and close to being admitted to a long-term palliative care facility. And, her older brother, Brian, had died suddenly in a house fire. I learned all of this very quickly in one of our first reconnecting conversations. I remember feeling shocked about her brother but not truly comprehending the depth of her loss. And a couple of years later, when we attended the funeral for the brother of another mutual friend, I remember feeling the most sympathy for his surviving spouse and our friend's elderly parents. I did not really think about how difficult it was for our friend to have lost her younger brother. I had no sense of the layers of loss that entwined for her. If one believes that life presents one with lessons to be learned, these two experiences were forerunners for what awaited. Less than two years later—almost to the day— Brent died.

> "Stephen, come now," I wail into the phone. . . . "It's not good. Please come now." "Okay," he says. Then I hear it. I still hear it even after all these years. A scream. One that reaches beyond your soul. I turn the corner. I know what the doctor has just said to Susanne and is going to say again. But when she says it, I still drop to the floor. "But he's only 38," I sob. "It was just the flu." She shakes her head and the nurse makes me drink some orange juice. The doctor disappears. The nurse kneels down and gathers me close to her. "We don't know why these things happen. They just do. And there are no regrets. Okay. It doesn't matter if you had any arguments or sadness. Never any regrets." (Brenda, personal story, 2008)

Karen came to Brent's visitation at the funeral home and met with me a couple of times over the next few months. She seemed to deeply understand how I felt and let me talk and cry and talk some more. Later, as the idea for a research project formed, Karen quickly volunteered to be a part of it. When we sat down for our first research conversation, more than 18 months had passed since Brent's death. I wondered how the conversations would impact us, if they would flow easily or if they would be punctuated with grief and sadness. I also wondered how it would impact our friendship.

As we met throughout that summer I came to know Karen and her brother Brian on a different level. She was still the kind person I remembered, always thinking and doing things for others but there was now a sadness present in our conversations. And, just as she had been the front runner for all the happy adult events awaiting us, she also suffered yet another first among our group of friends with the sudden death of her father in the midst of our scheduled interviews. I only found out when I arrived for our scheduled meeting and noticed flowers in her home. She had not wanted to interrupt what we were doing or put me in what she called an "awkward" position, so she had said nothing. The funeral had already passed. Her father's death was sad on many levels but most acutely as another milestone experienced without her brother Brian. As she put it, "I know I would have written a way funnier eulogy if he'd been with me. I just thought, 'Why do I have to do this without him?' He should have been here" (Karen, August 15, 2008).

Our friendship made the conversations easier. We moved seamlessly back and forth between our respective stories. It was comforting to talk to someone who knew Brent, as I think it was easier for her to be with someone who knew Brian. As our conversations drew to a close, I felt sad that we would not meet together as frequently. I had looked forward to our meetings as they were always mixed in with stories about her children and family. There was a blending of old and new lives that made it easier to talk about the sad parts. And, as with Rena, we laughed a lot.

MY BIG BROTHER

My grandmother bought us these helium balloons. Brian and I were playing a game where we tied a tennis ball to the string and watched it float. Of course the ball quickly fell out of the string and the balloon took off into the sky. I remember Brian looking through binoculars and giving me updates about where it was. "It's passing over Woolco plaza. It's over the ocean now," he said. "It's heading to Europe." I thought, wow, is he ever smart. He knows geography! (Karen, June 15, 2008)

Karen was the youngest of three siblings. Brian was two and half years older and her sister, Marny[1], eight years older. I always assumed Karen's strongest relationship was with her sister; however, as we talked I learned that it was actually Brian with whom she had shared the deepest connection. I knew Brian from when we were kids. Because he was older I never really spoke with him much but I remember just how much alike they were. The family resemblance was striking. They had the same eyes, facial structure and, as I came to learn as we talked, the same "essence." Karen recalled that as children, they were often mistaken for twins. Whether it was the closeness in age, or obvious genetic similarity, they formed a tight team and it was with him that Karen found her strongest ally. She thought of Brian as her friend and protector, and the one with whom she could laugh the hardest. It was always the two of them out shovelling snow, ganging up on her older sister, or just hanging around together.

When I was 17 I saved up all my money and went to visit him out in Edmonton. We had so much fun. We went out to a bar one night where they had these telephones on each table. Brian and I spent the night making crank calls to other tables, and we just laughed our heads off. I'm sure everyone thought we were crazy. (Karen, June 1, 2008)

Brian left home early, eventually following the building boom of the 1980s to Edmonton, where he worked in the trades. It was obvious as we talked about Karen's trip west how much she enjoyed their visit. "The two of us were young, and it was probably one of the times when we were the closest . . . because there were no wives, there were no boyfriends" (Karen, June 26, 2008). As we talked about that time I could tell that when the two of them were together there was an ease to their relationship that transcended anything they had with their friends. Brian made Karen feel very special, and all of his girlfriends knew the important place she

[1] Some details about Karen's family have been altered for this publication.

held in his life. There was a comfort and feeling of safety knowing her big brother was in the world and always available to look out for her.

When I asked Karen for words to describe Brian, the first one that came to mind was "gentle." He was someone who went through life simply going along with others, not wanting to make waves or needing to hold the spotlight. As a boy, he was "squished" between two sisters who took control of most of his socializing. And as an adult he found a partner who played a similar role. He simply "went along." She also described him as safety conscious, laughing as she said it. Karen recalled a family reunion where she arrived at the hotel only to find that her reservations had been canceled. Her brother had arrived first and quickly decided that it was not safe enough for the children. There were several baseball teams staying at the hotel, and he was concerned that post-game celebrations would lead to drunken players wandering the halls. He canceled everyone's reservations and rebooked them all at a new location. Karen smiled at the memory. Her brother was looking out for her yet again.

Most of our meetings happened at Karen's home. She was most comfortable there. It took me a while to get used to the rhythm of the constant motion around us. The phone ringing, teenagers coming and going, a daughter's boyfriend and his dog arriving and needing to be fed. It was very different than any of the other interview settings, which were quiet and controlled. As we talked, though, I soon learned how this interplay of energy was something Karen loved and missed the most about her life with her brother. His energy, his three children, the chaos of family gatherings were things that Karen loved. When he died, all of that disappeared.

> Brian and Laurie [Brian's wife] always had Thanksgiving, my sister had Christmas, and we had Easter. I still remember that one Thanksgiving where we gave all the kids 'whoopee cushions.' It was crazy. Everyone was screaming. I don't think I ever laughed so hard. And then there was that Christmas where we did a breakfast with Santa and we all stayed at this hotel. Brian went down to the pool with all the kids and we were supposed to follow and we didn't. Then we get this phone call, "Ah, does anyone care that I'm down here at the pool with seven children?" And we just laughed. (Karen, August 8, 2008)

Karen has no memory of holiday gatherings or even how she made it through each day during the first year after Brian died. What she does remember is an all-encompassing feeling of sadness and deep loneliness. Previously always a cheerful person, now her personality changed. She was angry and jealous of people who had living siblings, especially if they did not value the relationship. She resented being denied the opportunity to say good-bye to her brother and to tell him how she felt about him. She felt "ripped off." She took down all the family pictures. "I took them down just because they weren't . . . , they weren't part of my life anymore. . . . I thought if I just didn't have them up, then maybe I'd feel better" (Karen, June 26, 2008).

Brian and his family were previously a big part of Thanksgiving, Christmas, and Easter celebrations. Karen and her sister began inviting friends, extended family members, and neighbors to all the holiday meals to fill in the void. "I can't replace having his kids there, but there is a square and I'm trying to fit a circle in and it's kind of fitting, so it feels a little better" (Karen, August 8, 2008). Bringing unrelated family members into what were traditionally family gatherings changed the tone of the conversations. No one felt compelled to talk about Brian, which seemed to be the family's new way of coping. "The more people, the easier it is and then nobody has to talk about it" (Karen, July 24, 2008). Having a larger group satisfied a need to keep the conversation light and not bring up the obvious—that there was an entire family of five missing.

I have learned that the experience of grief is very personal; it often divides rather than unites families. Nowhere is this more noticeable than within a family as each member copes with the same loss differently. In our family, for the first few years, we stopped getting together as a group for many of the holidays. The first Thanksgiving after Brent died we gathered at Stephen's house. Susanne came with their children and we lit a candle in Brent's memory and later sat in a group and tried to share some memories. It was very hard though, and I remember my parents struggling to maintain their composure, almost as though hearing the stories was agony for them. We did not gather for Thanksgiving again for several years after; it was just too painful. For birthdays, we try to combine them, and for the last two summers have met at Stephen's home for a meal. Brent died on my dad's birthday, so we now let that day pass without any acknowledgment for my dad or for Brent. It is so hard to know what to do.

"I know it's cold but I bet you can put your tongue on that aerial." I did and of course it got stuck. "Statistically, it never happens to someone twice in a row. It's a fact," Brian said to me very calmly in his big brother voice. I did it again. He was wrong. (Karen, June 28, 2008)

"It's like you end up living the default" (Karen, July 24, 2008). You live with what is left and simply try to make the best of it. That means, in many cases, creating a new relationship with surviving siblings with whom you may not have previously been as close. Brian's absence forced closeness between Karen and her sister, which is comforting on some levels and yet feels artificial on others. It was Brian with whom she really felt connected, and so there is a quiet tension about their "new" relationship. They both know that it has deepened only because of Brian's death. This is complicated by the knowledge that the relationship between Brian and Karen's older sister was not a strong one. Karen finds it difficult to talk about Brian with Marny and so never does. She knows how her sister felt about her brother when he was alive. It makes it virtually impossible to have a conversation about him in death as she feels their grief over his loss is just so different.

Stephen and I are closer since Brent's death, but it does not replace what either of us has lost. My connection with Brent began in childhood when, as an older sister, I cared for him. He was the first person I felt responsible for, and that feeling of protectiveness was an ongoing theme in our relationship. We spent lots of time together as children, and as young adults our relationship continued to develop. We played on sports teams together, walked our dogs together, went mountain biking, and talked most days. He was my confidante and counselor, and we used to laugh at so many of the same things. I shared a different relationship with Stephen. We did not grow up socializing with one another as much and so do not have the same foundation of shared stories to draw upon now. I know he also had a special relationship with Brent. They played hockey on the same teams, went fishing together, and took ski trips. I cannot replace that connection for him anymore than he can replace mine with Brent. Brent was the hub in the wheel of our family, and with him now gone we must reform what we mean to each other.

To an outsider, Karen and Marny appear to be very closely connected. They socialize together often and talk on the phone regularly. They work together to jointly shuffle their collective teenagers to jobs and other after-school obligations. And even though Karen sees Marny more often than she saw Brian, and they do more activities together, it does not replace the lost connection. She still longs for the special feelings she shared with her brother.

FAMILY PAIN

> It was just easier to have two [services]. My parents were distraught, blaming Laurie for leaving him alone. So we had a memorial at their church, and then we jumped in the car and drove out to the memorial Brian's wife was having in Peterborough. It was so hard. She had left him just weeks before. Took the kids, said terrible things to him . . . had hurt him so much. I kept quiet and just went along with everything. I did it for him. (Karen, June 15, 2008)

Karen's relationship with her parents changed almost immediately after Brian's death. Karen and her sister organized a separate funeral to ensure that their parents would not have to interact with his estranged wife. Their anger at her for leaving the marriage, likely a normal reaction in any break-up, was magnified by Brian's sudden death. Karen felt extra pressure to ensure Brian's funeral included elements that might offer some measure of comfort for her parents. In speaking about her two daughters' and her nieces' involvement she said, "We made them sing this song from camp that had actions . . . and I remember Rachel saying, 'I don't even know the words, why am I doing this?'" I told them to "just do it . . . because it looks good for the family . . . and it will make Grandma and Grandpa happy" (Karen, July 24, 2008).

She continues to feel responsible for trying to "manage" her parents' pain. Immediately after Brian died she removed the video of his wedding from her parents' home, afraid her mother would watch it and ruminate over his death. Karen did the same with the cassette recording of her brother's funeral. Over the years her mother has asked for it many times, and Karen simply avoids giving it to her, telling her that it is put away or she will get it next time. She knows she will never give it to her and yet this is a conversation that is avoided. "It's almost like I think I'm protecting her, but who am I to think that I am protecting her?" (Karen, June 26, 2008). Not only do they avoid talking about Brian, they avoid having conversations about the real reasons why Karen does

Figure 17. "Day-Timer."
Source: B. Marshall, 2009.

(This is Brian's Day-Timer. It was in his truck parked away from the home
so it escaped the fire. Everything in it is exactly as Karen found it.
As she held it she remarked that she could still smell the scent
of his cigarettes.)

not want to give her mother the video or the cassette. Her mother's
grief and anger about Brian's death permeates their interactions,
and Karen believes watching the video or hearing the cassette will
make it even worse.

After Brian's death, her father's multiple sclerosis worsened and
he sank into a deep depression. He remained at home for the first few
years, his medical condition gradually worsening. Karen found it
hard to visit him as he became increasingly more despondent about
losing his son. He had been a distant parent all through Karen's
life and listening to him review his own behavior and sob in regret
was difficult for her. Eventually, he was placed in a long-term
care facility, and it was there that he died very unexpectedly one
evening. I had the feeling that her father's death came as a relief
for Karen. He was one less person for whom she had to try and
help manage their grief.

In addition to feeling responsible for her parents' mental well-
being, after Brian's death she took on more of the social connecting
responsibilities within the family. She became the "point person,"
called upon to handle everything that came up. She was the one

notified by the police about her father's sudden death and had to inform her mother and sister. When her mother was invited for special occasions with family friends, Karen now accompanied her. Taking on these new roles came at a cost. I perceived an underlying resentment that her extra contributions were unnoticed. She was simply expected to do everything.

In my family I also feel compelled to try and fill the void for my parents. I call them more frequently and visit more often. I still remember the pain in my mother's voice when she said, "First you notice the calls aren't coming anymore, and then you realize they won't be coming again," and then broke down into sobs. I felt helpless. At times the weight of this responsibility, self-imposed as it is, feels heavy. I try to compensate for Brent's absence, as though that were even possible. He used to call them a lot and, because he had children, he had stories about their lives that were interesting and upbeat. With him gone there is more time to fill, and my life and stories are not nearly as compelling. I often struggle with what to share, knowing that any attempt at recollecting stories that include Brent will cause them pain. I do not want to hurt them.

Webster Blank (1998, p. 18), herself a bereaved parent of an adult child, writes about the special difficulties elderly parents face when they lose a child. "It is late; life is winding down; they have less energy, flexibility, and resiliency to cope with the tragedy." In my view, no matter how old parents are when their children die, they struggle to continue parenting the remaining children. Almost instantly, the surviving adult children feel the need to step in and take over, our parents suddenly fragile and seemingly unable to cope. As children, we are not accustomed to seeing parents in this way. Within hours of Brent's death, Stephen and I were with Susanne making funeral arrangements. My dad was in the hospital recovering from major surgery and my mom was in a state of shock, having to care for my dad while at the same time trying to comprehend what had just happened to Brent. I remember driving her up to the florist in Barrie to meet Stephen so we could select flowers for the funeral. The day before, Brent was alive. I gently kept my parents informed about how the funeral would unfold, when the coffin would be open, what roles each was to play. At the visitation, when the line of visitors (which swelled into the hundreds) stretched outside and beyond the parking lot, I was the one asked to go and ask my parents to shorten their conversations with the people who had come to pay their respects. And, in the months that followed, I found myself acting as the bridge between them and Brent's wife, smoothing over disconnects and misunderstandings, just wanting everyone to be "okay." It was a very emotionally draining role to play and likely not one that anyone who has not been in this situation would ever imagine happens. Part of not speaking about our departed sibling comes from a desire to go along with however our parents have decided they wish to cope with the death of their child. If they do not want us to bring up their name, we do not.

Karen's mother cannot talk about Brian without being angry about the way he died. She blames his wife, certain that if she had not left him, others in the home would have noticed the fire that night. For similar reasons she lost contact with Brian's children, her grandchildren. Her bitterness cuts off any possible rejoicing in happy memories about Brian and limits what Karen can tell her about his children. She remains in a dark emotional place about his death, and Karen finds it easier to avoid the topic than face all the despair.

THE CHILDREN

> Oh my God, they'll have nothing. How will they remember their father? Everything is gone. The house was burned to the ground. There was absolutely nothing left. Even his car was burned beyond repair. I immediately started going through all of my pictures. I put together a box for each of them and shipped them out right away. (Karen, July 15, 2008)

Karen's immediate concern after the fire was for Brian's children. They did not attend their father's funeral, a decision made by Brian's estranged wife. This decision is something that continues to trouble Karen today. "So my biggest worry is . . . someday it's going to hit them. Someday they're going to have a breakdown . . . and not that I wish it on them, but someday they're going to need to talk to somebody that's not their mom" (Karen, June 26, 2008). Karen resolved to stay connected with Brian's children, to be ready for that call. Even today, she continues to send them greeting cards, letters, and notes. She speaks on the phone with them and stays up to date on their lives. "The most important thing for me now is the healing of the kids" (Karen, June 26, 2008).

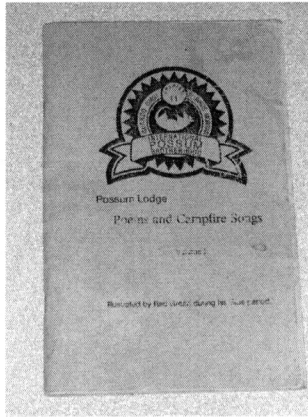

Figure 18. "Red Green."
Source: B. Marshall, 2009.

(Brian was at Karen's home a few days before he died in the fire.
He brought over this book, and she remembers him reading some of
the poems aloud and "laughing his head off." Red Green is a
fictional character on a television show.)
Retrieved May 29, 2009 from http://www.redgreen.com/

I know and understand this feeling and need to remain
connected. I want to support Brent's children in any way I can.
Brent was the kind of parent who got down on his hands and
knees to play with his children. Whenever his son was going
to party or a social occasion, they talked in advance about some
of the social rules. And then Brent would say, "and what's the
most important rule? 'To have fun,'" they would chime together.
It became known as "Daddy's rule." My desire to be an engaged
and active participant in their lives comes from wanting to
live "Daddy's rule," and maintain the link. The children were
devastated by their father's death. Even his 18-month-old daughter
would say "Daddy home now?" for weeks after. Susanne was
consumed with grief, just trying to keep the family on track.
Visiting during those initial weeks was my way of demonstrating
support and attempting to give the children moments of time
when grief was not the focus. I hoped I was a distraction. Like
Karen, I took on this responsibility willingly and gladly. Over time,

I have become a regular babysitter and the kids look forward to "adventures" with Aunt Brenda. Susanne builds time into their lives for me. They know I am their father's sister, and I like that our connection is important to all of us. When I am with Susanne and the children, "Daddy" is a regular part of our conversations. Our shared stories are comfortable, easy, and often joyful.

Brian's eldest daughter is soon to be married and Karen is considering a trip out West for the wedding. She has not seen her niece since the summer after Brian died. She returned to Ontario for a visit and Karen accompanied her to see the burned-out ruins of her home. I ask Karen what prevented her from visiting her nieces and nephew sooner. "I don't know. Maybe because I have no one to go with me," she replies. I can tell she feels pride in the accomplishments of her brother's children. One is attending university, one is to be married, and his son is doing well in high school. She also admires her sister-in-law for raising the children on her own. But, even as we talk about the positive changes in their lives, I still hear a sadness for the lost opportunity to be more involved. I feel lucky to have an opportunity to be part of Brent's family. For both Karen and me, the role of aunt was an important part of our identities. Karen loved being considered the "favorite aunt" and took great joy in planning events for everyone. Joining her family with Brian's was one of her favorite experiences, and to have lost all of them so suddenly was another layer of loss that was very painful. More than once she mentioned how others always noticed the physical resemblance between her niece and herself. That genetic connection through her brother was very strong.

REMEMBERING

I was pulling out place cards for Easter the other day and there are these Easter hats I'd made for Brian, his wife, and each of his three kids. I'd written each of their names on the front of their hat. I thought, come on, like, throw them out, like really, throw them out. But I put them back in the box. I don't know why I want to keep them. I just think that every Easter I'd like to open up the box and see them . . . and remember there was a time when we had Easters together . . . because you don't want to forget. (Karen, August 10, 2008)

"I think about him all the time . . . and it makes me angry if somebody forgets. 'Oh I didn't know you had a brother.' 'Yeah, I did'" (Karen, June 26, 2008). Even though it is seven years since Brian's death, Karen continues to miss him. She described it as a longing for everything to be in its place. She no longer feels whole—a piece is missing. In the first year after Brian died she felt a pressure to get over his loss quickly. Her family wanted her to be "normal." Her friends struggled to understand why she had changed and why she was so sad about Brian. It was only after seeing a counselor, at the insistence of her husband, that she began to feel a little better. "I think that somebody just had to validate the fact that I should be feeling that terrible and it was okay" (Karen, June 26, 2008). "I think that having permission to grieve makes you feel better because you think, well, maybe I shouldn't be feeling so bad, maybe I should be sucking it up. . . . I'm sure my mom's feeling worse, or maybe Laurie's feeling worse or . . . so I guess everybody should be feeling worse than me and so you kind of keep, just going and going and going, thinking, well, who am I to feel that bad" (Karen, July 24, 2008).

Karen's story about the Easter hats catches me every time I read it. It captures so well that feeling of deep, deep loss. A sibling knows the background to the family stories that are playing at any given time. With a glance, they understand all the weird family dynamics and instinctively know where those dynamics arose. Brian knew what the Easter hats meant. He knew the story behind the story.

Brian's death at such a young age, being "out of order," as Karen termed it, was something she mentioned many times in our conversations. "It wasn't the natural sequence that things should go, so do I keep on remembering him until the natural sequence isn't there?" she said. "Will it be okay finally when I'm 90? At least then it will make sense that he is gone" (Karen, June 26, 2008). Her father's sudden death in the midst of our interviews was difficult but not as impactful as the death of her brother. "I think it doesn't break my heart as much, because that's the natural sequence of life, whereas my brother should have been beside me. . . and he's not" (Karen, June 26, 2008).

Karen looked forward to the times when she and Brian would get together for weekends. The children were all the same age, which just added to the joy. The cousins loved each other and liked to be part of one another's lives. She pictured weddings, family gatherings, and continuing the circle for years to come. "It's like I have lost that one other person in the world who I could always count on. My relationship with my brother was beyond my relationship with my husband. We were the same genetics. The same blood. We had each other's backs. For always" (Karen, February 13, 2007).

MAKING MEANING

> I forgot about the time change so I woke up at six o'clock in the morning and I was so excited we were going to have a family reunion. I'm knocking on Brian's hotel room door, meanwhile it's four o'clock in the morning for them because of Alberta time. And he's laughing and yelling at me at the same time. Take the dog and get the hell out. We laughed about it later. (Karen, June 11, 2008)

In reflecting on our multiple conversations I saw Karen's meaning-making processes as a combination of tangible, active events that eventually evolved into more subtle changes about the way she viewed life. Initially, Karen focused her energies on trying to understand and integrate the facts of Brian's death into a scenario that made sense. There were subtle innuendos from others that perhaps the house fire was not accidental. "Was your brother depressed?" people asked. Brian was at Karen's home just days before the fire and she replayed that particular evening over and over, re-examining their conversation, looking for a trace of despair or depression that might provide some context for the fire. The idea that her brother might have taken his own life was upsetting and implausible. She invested hours tracking down, and then reviewing, the police and fire marshal's reports, reading between the lines, in order to make sense of the technical jargon. "I think part of it was just trying to figure out what happened and trying to make sense out of it" (Karen, June 26, 2008). Had he fallen asleep while smoking? Maybe alcohol was a factor? Or maybe an intruder had entered the home and Brian had died in a struggle? A few of Brian's possessions had survived the fire. One of them, his Day-Timer, became especially important as Karen went through it page by page, searching. "People say things about a fire, like, do you think it was accidental? And you're going, well, 'yeah,' and then you think, 'maybe there was a sign.' But there was no sign" (Karen, June 26, 2008). In the end Karen reconciled herself to the fact that it was an accidental

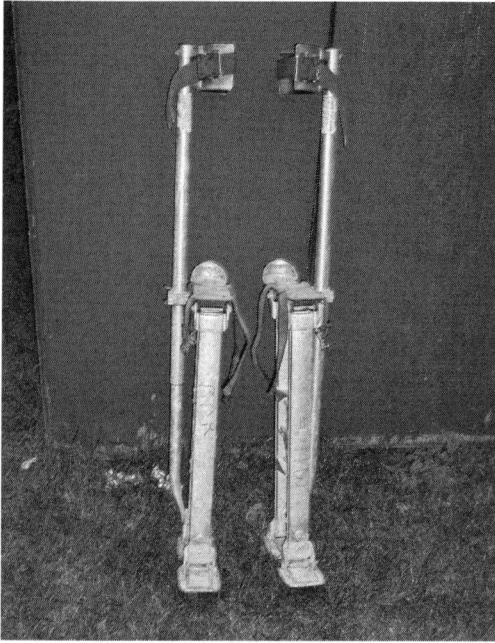

Figure 19. "Stilts."
Source: B. Marshall, 2009.

(These are Brian's stilts that he used when installing drywall on ceilings. As we looked at them, Karen noticed that his initials were engraved into the metal.)

fire—as all the reports indicated. There was nothing more to explore. While his death did not make sense from a "how life should unfold" perspective, she moved past the innuendos and accepted that the fire simply "just happened," as it does for countless families every day.

As a part of his funeral, grievers were invited to make donations to the Boy Scout troop to which Brian and his son belonged—a decision made by Karen. Camping and the outdoors was something that her brother loved, and this was a way of connecting his life with a positive activity in the present. The troop purchased new camping equipment with the donation and sent Karen a letter and badge commemorating the donation—something she kept in her memory box.

Karen also very quickly gathered together as many mementos as possible for Brian's children. It was important for her that they have something of their father beyond memories of their last few months together. Those months were filled with strife as Brian and his wife's marriage deteriorated. That Christmas, and for several to follow, she initiated a new tradition of sponsoring an underprivileged child, a boy, through a local charity. She and her daughters selected Christmas gifts specifically for him and although she never explained to her children why they did so, it was in memory of Brian.

As time passed, Karen developed ways to keep Brian's presence alive on a spiritual level. Most years she made it down to the Canadian National Exhibition to see Brian's old girlfriend. Because of the way things had ended with Brian's wife, Karen did not feel they could talk of shared memories. Sherry,[2] on the other hand, Brian's girlfriend before he met his wife, was someone with whom she could share happy memories about her brother. "It's a touch of him and knowing that somebody else didn't forget" (Karen, June 26, 2008). Being around someone who knew Brian well and loved him was comforting. Gradually she also began to share funny memories of her brother with her friends at work. There she could bring up a story and laugh without the awkwardness or pressure she felt when talking about him with family members. Karen's husband and children witnessed her deep despair when Brian first died and, thereafter, "walked on eggshells" whenever his name came up. Staying connected with his children, first through greeting cards and letters, and more recently through online social networking technology sites, also provided important connections. The recent birth of his grandchild was bittersweet. "Brian would have loved to be a grandfather," Karen said to me.

On another level, there were lessons that came out of Brian's death that Karen incorporated into her life. When I asked her about finding her way through the initial depression, Karen said she did not think her brother would have been happy seeing her so sad. "I think I just realized, slowly, very slowly, that he wouldn't have been happy with me behaving that way" (Karen, June 26, 2008). She also changed as a parent. She reinforced with her two daughters the importance of supporting one another. Karen wanted them

[2] Pseudonym for Brian's previous girlfriend.

Figure 20. "Badge."
Source: B. Marshall, 2009.

(This badge is from the Boy Scout troop to which Brian and
his son belonged. Karen made a donation in Brian's memory
after his death, and they sent her this badge along with
a letter of thanks.)

to understand that siblings were special, and she became upset
whenever her daughters fought with one another. She encouraged
her husband to reach out to his siblings. "Go, spend the day with
your brother because those days are important and you will never
forget those days" (Karen, July 24, 2008).

Brian was a kind person who always wanted people to get along.
Karen found that after his death she, also, became more empathetic
toward others. "I'm a lot more forgiving of people and I'm a lot . . .
more . . . I mean, I . . . I let things go. . . . I don't ever want someone
to leave me or to walk away from me and then life changes and
it's never the same" (Karen, June 26, 2008). In the past, where
petty disagreements may have annoyed her, now, those same things

simply did not matter. She also found herself more willing to reach out to others. This was especially true when she heard about someone whose loved one had died. Whereas before she might have procrastinated about sending a sympathy card, now she picked up the phone and called and made a point of writing a short note in a card. She was the first to volunteer to help at various church functions, cooking meals, organizing events, and being willing to help out—always saying "Yes." "His principles and his theories and his . . . his kind of life you know, these are the things . . . I've learned; I need to respect that . . . because I think he was a good person and I think that his heart was in the right place" (Karen, August 8, 2008).

When I asked Karen if she felt she was somehow better for having gone through this, she said "No," for that would be like saying Brian's death was acceptable. There was no "balance sheet" that could ever make things right. "I think I've resigned myself [to the fact] that it will never make sense" (Karen, August 8, 2008). I understood her reaction on a personal level. For even though there are things that have happened since Brent's death that are positive and uplifting, like the relationship I now have with his family, I would give it all back to have him alive and able to live his life. Having said that, though, a big part of re-establishing my own operating principles or equilibrium has come from taking steps, and making changes, that extend positive energy into the world. And although Karen did not label it as such, I believe that this was what she was doing also.

Karen talked about a heightened sense of intuition for people who needed help. She called them little "twings,"[3] fleeting thoughts about taking action or calling someone that she used to believe came from nowhere. Now, though, she believed they were coming from Brian. "And now when I have a 'twing' I believe that I know where it's coming from . . . I think he gives me nudges . . . they're never a mean-spirited nudge" (Karen, August 8, 2008). We had an example of this just before our interviews began. I carry a Blackberry communication device with me everywhere I travel. Five minutes before my scheduled presentation on Sibling Loss at the ADEC conference (Marshall, 2008) I happened to glance at it. Karen sent

---

[3] Karen invented this word to describe her feelings. It is pronounced as it is spelled: twings.

me a message inviting me for dinner and wondered how I was doing. I had not yet begun my research, and she did not know I was in Montreal. This was one of those moments where she felt like Brian had given her a message to reach out.

I saw the personal changes that Karen made in her life, especially regarding how she dealt with others in pain, as being one of her primary methods of re-ordering the way she operated in the world. Being able to help others in distress, to reach out and be kind to someone who needed comfort, was a way of honoring all the good things Brian brought to her world. She still missed him, still longed for his presence at family events, but found a way to integrate his spirit into her living world. And being part of this research gave her a chance to reconnect with happy memories about Brian in a tangible way. It also gave voice to the deep loss she felt and created a new opportunity to talk about her brother.

REFERENCES

Marshall, B. J. (2008, April). *Adult sibling loss: Disenfranchised grief and the sibling connection.* Paper presented at annual conference of the Association for Death Education and Counselling, Montreal, QC.Marshall, B. (2009).

Marshall, B. (2009). *Silent grief: Narratives of bereaved adult siblings* (Doctoral dissertation, University of Toronto, Toronto). Available from University of Toronto Research Repository. (http://hdl.handle.net/1807/19153)

Webster Blank, J. (1998). *The death of an adult child: A book for and about bereaved parents.* Amityville, NY: Baywood.

Catherine and James

Figure 21. "Siblings."
Source: Family Photo, Catherine, 1960s.

JAMES
(September 3, 1962—August 15, 2000)

> I just felt this sensation that, for whatever reason, I needed to get home, like a panicky feeling inside. I pulled up to my house and every light was on and I wondered "What the hell was going on?" I had just missed the police coming to the door. (Catherine, July 3, 2008)

"I'm on my third round of antibiotics for Strep" I heard her say to another participant. I froze. Instantly, my professional and personal worlds collided. I was in the midst of delivering a management education workshop, my first attempt at public speaking since Brent died, and I was working hard to compartmentalize my grief. My role as a facilitator was complex. I needed to engage people, teach new

Figure 22. "James."
Source: Family Photo, Catherine, early 1990s.

skills, and connect the content of the workshop with the participants' day-to-day realities. The client expected me to be in top form. There was no room for sadness, so I tried my best to create a mental divide between the "before" and "after." Brent was simply away. I constantly reminded myself not to cross over for, if I did, I knew it would release a flood of emotions that would be hard to control. And yet, with this casual comment, my internal façade was broken and I fought to keep the memories of Brent's last hours out of my mind.

By chance, on the next break, I found myself alone with Catherine in the hall. "You best be careful with that strep," I said. "It's a nasty bug, it can be very serious." And then I added, "My 38-year-old brother just died six weeks ago from it." I do not know why I disclosed this fact. It was probably my way of bringing Brent into my living world that particular day. I think by trying so hard to force him out of my consciousness I was fighting the natural order of things. Catherine's answer shocked me. "My 38-year-old brother died too— five years ago." I gasped. "He was found in a river at the bottom of a bridge. We don't really know what happened. I still feel bad because I wasn't there. All my life I took care of him and yet at that one moment, when he needed me the most, I wasn't there."

The workshop continued with both of us sharing parts of our stories on breaks. At the end of the day Catherine gave me her business card and invited me to call. I was struck by the synchronicity of our meeting and kept her card in a safe place. More than a year and half later, when I had long since resigned from the role that took me to her company, I sent her a note. We met for lunch, and I told her about what I was planning. She quickly volunteered and within months our interviews began.

MY LITTLE BROTHER

> I remember walking with my brothers to Sunday school. My brothers would take off after the fire engines, and I would go to class. They'd meet back up with me on the way home so it would look like the three of us all went. I never told on them. They only went on days where they got something—like Easter where they got a chocolate egg or Christmas when there was candy. I was the responsible one who went all the time. (Catherine, August 13, 2008)

We met at Catherine's office, usually her first appointment of the day. I wondered how meeting at her workplace would influence

Figure 23. "Shirt."
Source: B. Marshall, 2009.

(This shirt belonged to James. In the pocket is a small slip
of paper with a phone number on it.)

our conversations. As someone familiar with corporate life I anticipated frequent interruptions. I also wondered what it would be
like for Catherine to move from talking about her brother back
into business mode without a break in between. With the other
participants, we always met on days when they did not have obligations immediately after in case our conversations proved to be
emotionally difficult. I worried about the impact of trying to fit my
conversation with Catherine into what, otherwise, was a very busy
day. From my experience, the workplace was not a place that welcomed
these kinds of conversations.

Our interviews, however, progressed easily throughout the
summer and into the fall. Catherine's office was very quiet and we
were never disturbed. She remained calm and composed throughout,
her answers factual and direct. It seemed like she had already spent
a lot of time thinking about her brother and her own emotional

reactions to his death. By the time of our first meeting I was just finishing interviews with Karen and Rena, and the essence of their collective stories became part of my conversations with Catherine. I sometimes interjected experiences the others revealed, or ones from my own life, which often prompted new stories. I felt comfortable talking with Catherine. There was something about our shared loss of a younger sibling, a little brother, that connected us in a unique way. We both knew what it meant to feel responsible.

> The bell rings. It's 1:25 p.m. and everyone is lining up to go into class. I look toward the junior kindergarten area of the playground—the place where I had dropped Brent off just a few minutes before—my job of getting him safely to school complete. And yet, there he was, running away from all the others going into class. He took one last look at me, smiled, and then was gone. My 8-year-old brain was faced with such a terrible dilemma. Do I go after him or do I go into class? "Brenda, let's go," my teacher called. (Brenda, personal story, November 2008)

I remember that day like it was yesterday. I fretted about Brent for the rest of the afternoon, looking out the window of my classroom, hoping to see him returning. I could not wait for the school day to end, at which point I raced home to find him happily riding his bike outside. Apparently he wandered into the local doctor's office and spent the afternoon playing with toys in the waiting room. After a while the receptionist realized he was there alone and called my mom to come and get him.

> When I was in grade 2 the teacher invited me up to the front of the class to sing a song for everyone. Well, I guess I liked it too much because I refused to sit down and soon found myself standing in the hall. I remember looking down toward the kindergarten room, and there's my little brother, standing out in the hall too. The two of us both in trouble at the same time! (Catherine, July 31, 2008)

Like me, Catherine grew up feeling a deep sense of duty or responsibility to keep her younger brother safe. There were four siblings[1]— an older brother, Catherine, James, and then a much younger sister. Catherine described herself as her "father's favorite" and her brother

---

[1] Some details about Catherine's family have been changed for this publication.

James as "my favorite." A troubled child, James was constantly in battles in the playground and in the classroom. Catherine quickly established herself as his protector, charging into groups of kids to save him at recess, never fearing for her own safety. Her protective arms continued to reach around him at home where his challenging behaviors were often met with punishment, anger, and misunderstanding. "I think I loved him or felt I had to—because no one else did" (Catherine, August 2008).

She described her family life as difficult. Both her parents came from "tough backgrounds" and had a hard time parenting, having had very poor role models themselves. They were even more ill equipped to handle a child who, from an early age, demonstrated behaviors that were out of step with other children of the same age. James was different. Looking back, Catherine now believes James likely suffered from undiagnosed ADD[2] or ADHD[3] and perhaps a learning disability. He struggled in school and was labeled a "bad kid." At home, her parents were very hard on him and she often intervened on his behalf. "He was always needing to be taken care of. He was always in trouble or something" (Catherine, July 31, 2008). Feeling responsible for James was a theme in all our conversations. Catherine felt very strongly that it was her role to step in and help him; she just knew no one else would do so. She saw herself as his only real ally, the one person who understood and loved him unconditionally. "And still to this day, I feel that I really was the only one who truly cared for him the way he deserved to be cared for" (Catherine, July 31, 2008).

THE DARK SIDE

I saw him grasp at finding different things in his life. At one point we got a phone call from him and he was in a donut shop in Niagara Falls. He had hopped into a truck with this musician who was going to hit the big time in New York City. By Niagara

---

[2] ADD, or attention deficit disorder, is a term used to describe a pattern of behaviors seen in children who often struggle with learning. The Canadian Mental Health Association has a very informative website with additional information on this disorder. Retrieved March 3, 2009, from http://www.cmha. ca/BINS/content_page.asp?cid=3-99

[3] ADHD, or attention deficit and hyperactivity disorder, is similar to the above with an added component of poor impulse control. Additional information may be found at the website noted above.

Falls she had run out of money. She went in to use the washroom and took off on him. So it was this whole series of people just, you know, not coming through for him and so we brought him back to our house and tried to convince him to stay in Ontario. We'd help him get a job, and all of that, but he wanted to go back to Calgary and that was the last time I saw him. (Catherine, July 31, 2008)

When James was in his teens, he moved out West with his high school sweetheart. He was a talented photographer and, for several years, seemed to do very well. When his marriage disintegrated, it sparked a slow slide into a very dark life, eventually finding him leading a hand-to-mouth existence. Catherine recalled this time as difficult. She often received long rambling phone calls from him at odd hours of the night. Privately, she wondered if he was suffering from a mental illness or perhaps had fallen victim to substance abuse. His life seemed out of control, and she worried about him constantly. "We were really close. Of all my siblings he's the one that I mothered" (Catherine, July 31, 2008).

"He would always have these big ideas—great big ideas—and then the next day he would be really down about that great big idea that was so awesome the day before" (Catherine, July 31, 2008). I asked Catherine if she ever felt frustrated by her brother's inability to carry things through. She replied that she was always "in his corner" and felt it was her role to be supportive hoping that, at some point, things would "come together." It was one of those big ideas that brought James to Niagara Falls that day years ago. Catherine looks back on that time sadly, feeling like it was the fork in the road that could have changed the outcome. "I guess I very much had that . . . feeling for him, like I would have done anything to protect him" (Catherine, August 13, 2008). She drained her bank account, giving him everything. Years later, she found out her younger sister had done the same. They wondered what happened to the money they gave him. Even now, eight years later, Catherine is still tortured that she did not do more to help him. "We should never, ever have let him go back and should have recognized that something was seriously wrong with him and taken action to help him sort his life out" (Catherine, October 4, 2008).

We were the explorers. We would get up in the morning and we'd be gone. On a weekend we'd pack a paper bag lunch, and off we'd go exploring in the Don Valley and parks nearby. We'd get on the streetcar and go to the Toronto Zoo, which was the Riverdale Zoo at that time. And then we'd go visit my

> grandmother who lived in Cabbagetown all by ourselves, and we
> were about 9, 7, 5 years old. As long as we were home by the
> time my mom was calling us for dinner, that's all they cared
> about. (Catherine, July 31, 2008)

Catherine smiled as she recounted this story. I could tell how much she enjoyed the memory of romping around Toronto with her brothers. Like me, she grew up at a time when children had lots of freedom to come and go. As they grew older Catherine and her brothers shared friends, having big parties in their home with everyone bringing along their own group. The traits that provided James challenges as a child only added to his personality as an adult. Catherine described him as "funny, off-the-wall, different, very extroverted" (Catherine, October 4, 2008). He was someone who "lit up a room" and collected friends wherever he went. I had this impression that he was the ultimate party guest, comfortable talking to anyone, and full of fun and interesting stories.

She remembered a trip out West when he took Catherine and her husband "off roading" in his Jeep. They plunged through a river in the back country, water leaking in through the doors, her brother laughing the whole time. There was nothing that frightened him; he loved the adrenalin of the adventure. At the time, he lived in a small, simple home that Catherine described as something like "the run-down home on the old hit television series Green Acres" (Sommers, 1965). Sheets for curtains, walls needing painting—very basic conditions were all that he needed. James did not put on airs or need to have things look a certain way. Everyone was welcome at his home at any time. The connection she felt to him was evident.

I felt a similar connection with Brent. As a child, I kept a medical dictionary under my bed. When Brent wasn't feeling well he would come to me and, together, we would look up his symptoms in my book. "I think you have either . . ." and I would list off all the possibilities. He was on his way with his children to watch me compete in a triathlon when he first felt ill. He never made it to my race, instead, calling to let me know something was wrong. We talked every day that next week, and I began to worry that he was not getting any better. I convinced him to go the hospital. He went, following my advice like he always did. They hydrated him and sent him home with "the flu." A few days later he was dead. Although I never felt like a mother to Brent, I realize now how much I enjoyed being his "big sister," the one who he came to for advice. I think I miss mattering to someone, the way I mattered to him.

As I got to know Catherine better, I learned she, like James, shared a love of the arts. They were both creative in their own ways. He loved photography. She loved decorating, acting, and being a part of her daughter's singing career. I asked if she thought this similarity contributed to the special connection they shared. Within their family, they were the only two who had artistic leanings. She had not thought about this before but acknowledged that she and James communicated in a way that transcended words, almost telepathically. And perhaps, their connection as artists contributed to that ability.

LAST DAY OF NORMAL

So my husband said to me, "Well, your brother was found dead." Of course, I have two brothers, right? So, my gut reaction is, "Which brother?" I remember saying, "Which brother?" And then I was . . . just comatose after that. I was just numb. I wanted right away to talk to my older brother and I remember saying, "Call my brother. Call my brother," and he kept saying, "Are you okay? Are you okay?" I told him to phone my brother because I needed to know . . . in my mind, I needed to make order of this. (Catherine, July 31, 2008)

Catherine boarded a plane westward the next day and, with her mother, brother, and sister made the funeral arrangements. As I write the words "funeral arrangements," I realize they are a comfortable way of compressing what were likely some of Catherine's most difficult days into a couple of words. She wanted to see James—a memory she holds with both gratitude and regret. "In some ways, I regret doing that [seeing his body] but, in other ways, I'm so glad that I did because I would have always wondered, 'what if they got the wrong guy'" (Catherine, July 31, 2008). She later went to his apartment to pick up his few belongings. Too distraught to speak at the service, her teenage daughter delivered a eulogy. Afterwards she recalls simply feeling numb. "It was an overwhelming grief for me" (Catherine, August 13, 2008). There was a deep sense of guilt over how her brother's life had turned out. She felt there she could have done more to help him and wondered why someone so special died so tragically. Always his protector, she felt she had let him down in his most desperate moment.

For a long time afterward it was difficult to function. An entry from Catherine's journal, reprinted below, describes her deep sadness. Reading this is like seeing a page from my own journal, so strikingly similar are the words.

> It's been almost six weeks since James died and still it has not sunk in. I keep forgetting and then remembering with such a jolt that my heart leaps. I will never see or talk to him again. I feel this huge, deep sadness inside that I can't make my way out of. I take pills every night to sleep and am terrified of lying awake in the darkness. How do you keep going and pull yourself out? The days are easier than the nights—I can keep busier. I have a sense that no one really understands that I am dead inside. (Catherine, personal journal, October 2, 2000)

The sadness Catherine felt and continues to feel mirrors that of the other participants. Each one expressed the overwhelming nature of their grief, consuming them beyond what they felt anyone could possibly understand. It was a never-ending dark place; something only another bereaved sibling could feel. To me Catherine appeared to have a very full and satisfying life. Her children were grown up and doing exciting things with their lives. She had a varied and active career, and many outside interests kept her busy. And yet, she expressed an ongoing sadness. It was for herself but also for the life her brother never got to lead. He never got to feel like a winner and that was something that troubled her deeply. I gently asked if she thought there would ever be a point in her life when there would be enough going on that she would not feel his absence so acutely. "I don't think your heart, the piece that loved my brother, can re-grow and love somebody else instead" (Catherine, October 4, 2008).

As with Karen, Rena, and me, Catherine's other family relationships were strained after James died. In the early days of her grief, she felt angry at her mother for not helping her brother when he was small. She was angry at her older brother for not intervening when he saw James spiraling downward as an adult. And she felt very alone in her own family. Her strongest ties were with her brother James and her father. Her father died nearly 20 years earlier and, with them now both gone, she felt disconnected from everyone else. "They were bonds that I never ever had with anybody else. So I miss that . . . I feel like my family was taken away from me" (Catherine, August 13, 2008).

Catherine's anger reminded me of how I felt about a co-worker who was the same age as Brent. He was more than a colleague; he was my friend. I liked that he had children the same ages as Brent's children. We used to chat about them and, like Brent, he was in sales and was fun to be around. Unlike Brent, though, work seemed to be the place where he felt most alive and he worked very long hours, confiding in me that he knew he was short-changing his family. After Brent died, watching him continue to "short change" his family became increasingly difficult. It troubled me deeply that he did not spend time with his children. Even on his days off he found a way to get involved in our business dealings. I began to resent him for having the chance to do everything that my brother could now never do. It all seemed so unfair. I am sure my colleague had no idea why I stopped talking to him and began to avoid him at the office. I did not understand it myself until I wrote these words about Catherine.

As time progressed, Catherine's relationship with her remaining siblings and her mother changed. Her older brother, with whom she had already begun to grow distant from before James died, now felt like a stranger. Since the day she flew home from his funeral they have not spoken about James. Neither does she speak with her mother about him. "You kind of feel your way around and you get to know subconsciously what you do and don't talk about" (Catherine, July 31, 2008). Catherine has thought a lot about how the other members of her family dealt with James's death. She concluded that part of their ongoing communication struggles came from how differently they had all experienced and expressed grief about James's passing. It drove a wedge between them all, something I experienced in my own family, an experience with which both Rena and Karen concurred.

"For me, because of the closeness of our relationship, I guess it was very much like losing a child" (Catherine, July 31, 2008). The revelation that in many ways James had felt like a child to Catherine came during our interviews. After each meeting I sent Catherine a transcript of our interview. We began the subsequent meeting by talking about the themes raised in the previous conversation. "I didn't realize how . . . much I thought of him as almost a child to me and how . . . my relationship kind of transcended sister to more of a mothering role" (Catherine, August 13, 2008). She was surprised by the number of references she made to "needing to take care of" her brother. As she described her life growing up it was as though she had stepped in to fill a gap for her brother. She watched him struggle, telling me "he was always on the short end of the stick" his whole life. "I feel that I was the only one who ever really loved him" (Catherine, July 31, 2008). With his death, she wanted to see some expression of remorse or guilt from her mother, an acknowledgment of the role she might have played in the way his life had turned out. At the same time though, she chose not to directly confront her mother about this or force a conversation about James. Karen and Rena both felt compelled to try and protect their parents from further grief. While I did not hear those same sentiments from Catherine, she did choose to protect her mother from her own angry feelings about what had happened.

MAKING MEANING

He had this old metal horse and buggy. It was very small, built for a 2-year-old. Anyway, James carted it around with him and kept it for all those years. And then something bad

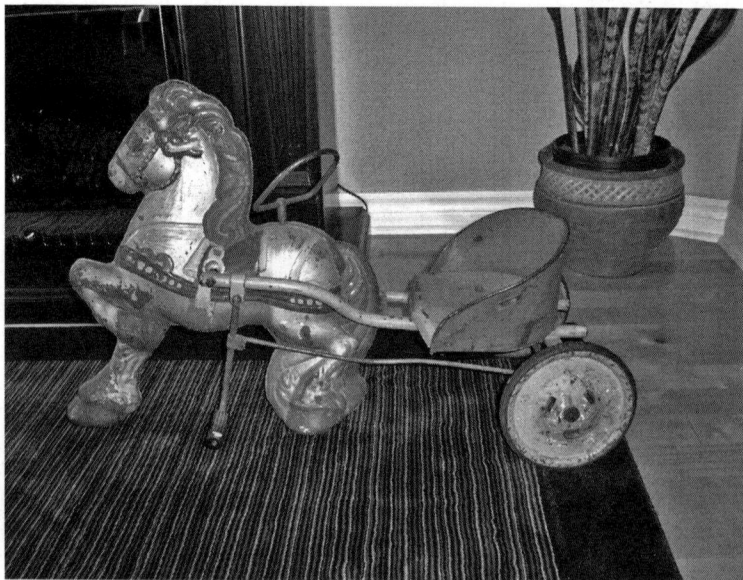

Figure 24. "Horse & Buggy."
Source: B. Marshall, 2009.

must have happened because he took it to the pawn shop. It was sitting in the window. When he died his friends went and bought it back and gave it to us. I have it here in my living room. It mattered to him, so it matters to me. (Catherine, October 4, 2008)

As I discovered in my conversations with Karen and Rena, the concept of meaning making is multilayered. For Catherine, there was meaning that needed to be made around the events leading to James's death. What actually, physically, happened to him? And, contextually, what were the circumstances that lead to him being on that bridge at that time? Similar to Karen, Catherine poured through technical paperwork from local authorities with the purpose of making sense of the details. Her brother's death was listed as "suspicious" and yet there was no further investigation. Although found in a river, he had not drowned, and there were signs of trauma to his body. "You see these investigative shows where they spend all this time caring about how somebody died and then in real life it doesn't happen that way" (Catherine, July 31, 2008). She went to the bridge, walked down to the water, and looked up. There was nothing that he could have hit. Not satisfied with what she read and heard, she had his medical reports reviewed by an Ontario coroner. Had he been hit by a car and then fallen over? Perhaps he had been in an argument and then been tossed over? Or, she wondered if he had deliberately jumped. The corner indicated there were signs of trauma and left it at that. She resigned herself to the fact that she would never know what really happened that night. It was clear though from our conversations, that even eight years later, she still felt guilty that she was not there to save him, as she had done so many times when he was a little boy.

Her brother's death started Catherine on a new path. After making her way through the deep depression that followed, she began rethinking everything in her life. "Am I happy in my marriage? Am I happy in my career? What am I doing to make my life more meaningful?" (Catherine, August 13, 2008). Looking back she believes she was depressed for about two years before she sought professional help. Similar to what Karen expressed, Catherine felt she had already suffered serious blows in life and did not understand why the universe was presenting yet another challenge. As a teen, her beloved grandmother was brutally murdered in her own home by a teenage neighbor. Her father, the parent with whom she

Figure 25. "Carving."
Source: B. Marshall, 2009.

(Catherine is not sure where this carving is from.
She wonders if James made it when he was a little boy.)

had felt most connected, had died when she was in her mid-twenties. "And then the harsh reality of losing somebody again, made me think, oh God, who knows, that life isn't fair and there's no rhyme or reason to why or how things happen. It just isn't fair" (Catherine, October 4, 2008).

Part of Catherine's meaning making was about coming to some conclusions about life; specifically, that the world really did not revolve around the concept of fairness, that "good" people lived long lives and "bad" people died early. "I think we come with a date stamp on our necks" she said to me many times during our conversations. For Catherine, part of restoring order was to formulate a new view and logic to explain her loved ones' deaths. Coming to believe that individuals were "date stamped," their deaths predestined, was an important layer in Catherine's restructuring of her belief system. By acknowledging that James's death was determined by a greater force, she accepted that it was not her responsibility to keep him alive. It was his time to go, and there was nothing she could do to change that. We talked about this concept several times during our conversations and, even though I felt Catherine wanted to accept James's passing as inevitable, I sensed that she continued to harbor guilt about it. During one of our last meetings I directly asked her about this and she acknowledged that part of her still felt she could have done something to change the outcome.

I asked Catherine if she kept any mementos of her brother. Initially she said "I don't have much." At the following meeting she described several of many objects she had, acknowledging her own surprise at finding so many. We both smiled. We decided to meet at her home so we could walk around and look at each item while we talked. I was immediately struck by the prominent location the mementoes had in her home. The horse and buggy was set in the middle of the living room. No one could sit in the room without commenting on it—thereby prompting a story about its origin and how it came to be. In her bedroom, a framed picture of his Jeep sat directly in front of her bed; the first thing she saw every morning. "This was his prized possession . . . he took that picture, because he loved this Jeep and it represented everything that he loved . . . that kind of encapsulates who he is" (Catherine, September 11, 2008). We meandered through her home and Catherine pointed out other small items. A silver flask, a small Indian carving, an urn created by an artist friend of her brother that had been delivered too late to be used at his funeral. Each item, carefully displayed in elegant cases, and each had a story. Even outside in the garden, Catherine placed a rock from the river where he was found. She liked having it close, like having her own private sanctuary. As we talked about each of the items that day, it seemed that Catherine was carrying on the attachment to these items on behalf of her brother. "I can't ask him what these meant to him but obviously they meant something, so I took everything that I could get because I felt . . . 'Who else would appreciate it?'" (Catherine, September 11, 2008).

There were three milestones that coincided with my meetings with Catherine. The first one was the marriage of Catherine's oldest daughter. As the day approached Catherine had mixed emotions knowing that both her brother and father would not be there. As a wedding gift to her daughter she had one of the few remaining photos taken by her brother turned into several pieces of art. She gave it to her daughter on behalf of James. Her daughter had eulogized

Figure 26. "Flask."
Source: B. Marshall, 2009.

(The significance of this flask is unknown.
It was found among James's belongings.)

him at his funeral several years earlier, and they had a special bond. There was also a memory table at the service for other loved ones who had passed away, and a donation in their memory was made to a local charity by the bride and groom. On this special day, Catherine kept her brother present.

Figure 27. "Urn."
Source: B. Marshall, 2009.

(This urn was created by an artist friend of James's.
It arrived too late to be used at his funeral. It is sitting
on a table just inside the entrance to Catherine's home.)

We also passed what would have been James's 46th birthday and the anniversary of his death. Like Karen, Catherine preferred not to treat the day as one of significance. "I don't really acknowledge it as a day different from any other day because I think about him all the time" (Catherine, August 13, 2008). I found it interesting that where both Rena and I attached great significance to the day our siblings died, both Karen and Catherine preferred not to do so. I wondered if it was because, for them, there were a lot of unknowns around their siblings' deaths and perhaps the last day of life was not seared in their memory. For both Rena and me there was a clear demarcation between "before and after." We were both at the hospital when our siblings took their last breaths; the line between life and death was clearer.

One day, I was coming along Highway 401 not far from here and the Louis Armstrong song—"What a Wonderful World"— came on the radio. They played it at his funeral and I started to tear up and I'm thinking, you know God, I never want to hear this song again. Then all of a sudden, the sun breaks out of the clouds . . . and this light comes down, like the sun, just beautiful sunshine. (Catherine, August 13, 2008)

Catherine described a new spiritual connection she had with her brother. He was not gone, just on another plane, where she could still speak with him. The only difference, now, she said was "he could not answer back." "I believe that you go onto another world, that he's on another plane of existence. We just can't interact. But he's there, he's with my dad, he's with his dog, whatever. He's still there" (Catherine, July 31, 2008). She recalled a visit with a psychic who told her that her brother was "happy and content." Once she heard that he was no longer in pain she was better able to integrate his death into her life. Although she continued to feel sad, she was comforted to know he finally found happiness. This realization was another turning point in her life. "And that was kind of the beginning of my road to feeling better about myself and everything that had happened" (Catherine, July 31, 2008). It was the beginning of looking at life through a different lens.

"It's given me a little more courage in my life to try to do some things that I may not have ever done. . . . I'm not going to leave any stone unturned" (Catherine, October 4, 2008). Part of the way Catherine has made new meaning in her life is by being "brave and adventurous." As I write those words I think of the story she told me of James racing his Jeep through the river. His excitement and zest for adventure has become hers. She has changed jobs many times, feeling the itch to move every few years. She took up acting, trying out for television commercials, even a reality show. "I am no longer afraid to simply try things," she said to me. "I've figured out how to go on and find joy in my life, but I think I'm always trying to find things to keep me finding joy" (Catherine, August 13, 2008).

She became more caring, especially, of the downtrodden, people on the street living moment to moment. "I am probably far more receptive to helping people in need. I have never looked at anybody else on the street the same way as I did before my brother died" (Catherine, October 4, 2008). James's sad spiral downward was a vivid reminder of how quickly life can change. It also emphasized for Catherine how difficult life can be for people who struggle with mental health issues. Today she no longer passes people on the street without handing them money. She looks beyond the figures sitting in front of her and wonders about their stories, what brought them to that point. Catherine also took this "message" of sharing into her parenting style. "Always be kind . . . always. Help people who are less fortunate than you. If you're lucky enough to have . . . wealth and happiness and everything in your life, share it. Because it's no good having it all alone," (Catherine, August 13, 2008) she told her children.

She learned to tell people she loved them and to be more open about her feelings toward others. The realization that people could be present one day and then, suddenly, gone was what propelled her to extend herself this way. "So if you want to go see that person you care about, you better go, because there's a possibility there isn't a tomorrow" (Catherine, October 4, 2008). Although their expressions of caring were different, I found it intriguing that both Karen and Catherine now seemed to operate from a place of immediacy when it came to reaching out to others. As soon as they had the slightest sense that someone needed help, they both reached out without delay. Similarly, they both made a point of encouraging their children to do the same. From our conversations I knew that this knowledge and new way of being in the world had not come immediately or easily for either Karen or Catherine. They went through a period of darkness before they began to find their footings in life again.

> "And why does it matter to you that there is a story about James that continues?" I think because he was a very special person. At least, he certainly was to me and I'd like the story told in my terms versus my older brother's terms or my sister's terms. Each one of us has different memories, and I'd like mine to be on record. (Catherine, October 4, 2008)

Like Karen, and Rena before her, Catherine was grateful for the chance to talk about her brother. She saw it as a way to tell and record the story of James's life so that she could pass it down through the generations. "This way, we have a family history. No one else is telling the story. As far as I am aware, there is no one else in my family that keeps a journal, or does anything like that, so when we're gone one day, everything will go with us" (Catherine, October 4, 2008). Our work together also gave her new opportunities to talk to people about James. At a recent corporate dinner she told colleagues about our interviews and the purpose of the research. A long conversation about her brother and his life followed where normally this would not have happened.

For Catherine, there were parts of James's life that she still struggled to integrate and accept. I could tell the harshness of his experiences as a misunderstood little boy and later as an adult, just slightly out of step with the world, were painful memories. "A bright star, who never got to shine," she said to me sadly. Perhaps that was why the psychic's words were so important for her. Finally, he was at peace. James's death was part of an accumulation of grief over other lost loved ones, and reaching some new understanding about the world and rules it operated by were important for Catherine. There was no balance sheet. There was no way to pay dues and thus be exempt from further grief. Deaths were predestined and there was nothing that could be done to change that.

REFERENCES

Marshall, B. (2009). *Silent grief: Narratives of bereaved adult siblings* (Doctoral dissertation, University of Toronto, Toronto). Available from University of Toronto Research Repository. (http://hdl.handle.net/1807/19153)

Sommers, J. (1965). *Green Acres.* {Television series]. Los Angeles, CA: Columbia Broadcasting System.

PART THREE

Themes

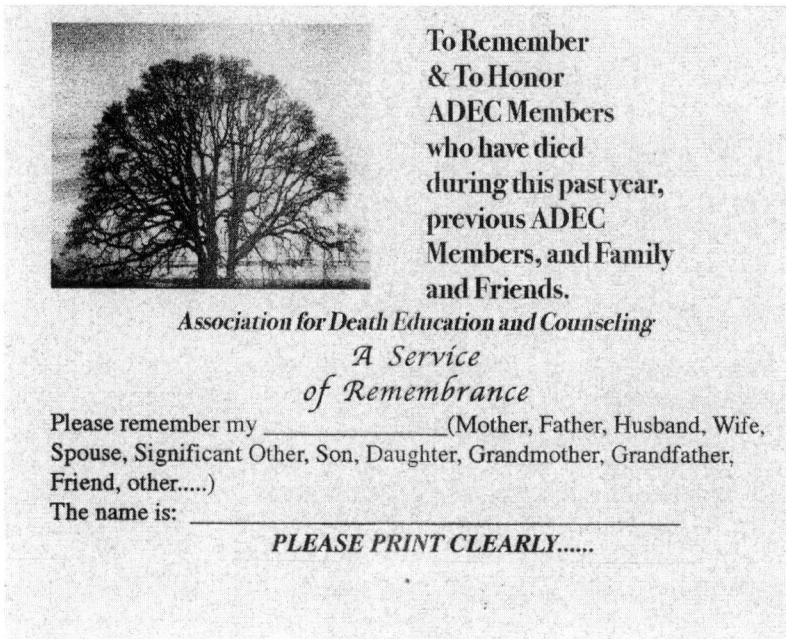

Figure 28. "ADEC Memorial Card."

At presentations, I often begin by projecting this image on the screen. "What's interesting about this card?" I ask. Bereaved siblings are the first to notice. "Mother, Father, Husband, Wife, Spouse, Significant Other, Son, Daughter, Grandmother, Grandfather, Friend, other . . ." are all mentioned. Siblings are not. When I explain that this memorial card was passed out at the 2008, 2009, and 2010

Association for Death Education and Counseling (ADEC) con-
ferences, events designed to attract experts in the field, the audience
often falls silent. This visual tells the story so well. Siblings (we)
are simply not on the card—of experts, friends, family, or society
at large. And this lack of acknowledgment, felt from the moment
after death, begins a cycle of what I've come to call "silencing." It
is noticeable in the early days when support is focused on other
family members and continues as conversations about our deceased
siblings are quickly dismissed and avoided among friends. Lastly,
it's there when we want to share happy stories and others find it
too difficult to listen.

Silencing amplifies the bereavement experience for many siblings
and while certainly not present for all, for those who do experience
it, the impact is profound. It causes many to wonder if they are
entitled to feel such intense grief. Others describe abject loneliness as they walk through their days feeling disconnected and
different from friends and colleagues. Others grow resentful of
happy sibling pairings or find it challenging to listen to friends
complain about living brothers and sisters. And finally, silencing
makes the process of reconnecting with our siblings in a new
way more difficult. There are few who let us celebrate our siblings
through stories and laughter.

My goal with this book was to explore the experience of sibling
loss through the collective vision of four bereaved siblings. True to
narrative practices, I wanted each story to stand on its own, and
leave readers to draw their own inferences and conclusions. And
while the narratives of Rena, Karen, and Catherine are different,
and their experiences of loss unique, there are common themes
that run across their stories that are powerful. I offer them here
not as "the truth" or representative of all siblings' experiences, but
as ideas for further reflection and discussion.

PROFOUND LOSS

It's a hole and you just can't fill it. You move on, you figure out
ways to [go on] but it's always going to be there. I'll tell you 10
years from now it will still be there. (Catherine, July 31, 2008)

I don't remember anything. I don't remember taking pictures
at Christmas, I don't remember Christmas shopping. I was
just beside myself. . . . It was the loneliest time of my life. (Karen,
June 26, 2008)

And sometimes I see sisters together having lunch or they're going shopping together or they're walking together or even in the hospital, sisters are with each other at appointments when they're elderly—and that was the way it was supposed to be. (Rena, July 2, 2008)

For all three women, their sibling's death was devastating. They used words like "hole," "missing piece," or "injury" to describe the pain and disfigurement they felt at the loss of such an important relationship. In the early days, they missed the phone calls, check-ins, and just the feeling of connection they had to their brother or sister. "I would come home from work and want to pick up the phone and call her, and suddenly I'd catch myself" (Rena, June 11, 2008). Rena spoke with her sister every day of her life, never missed a day visiting her in the hospital, and suddenly, she was gone. Karen refused to believe the human remains found in her brother's burnt-out home were his. Instead, she convinced herself he was simply away on a trip that he'd chosen not to tell his family about. She waited, delaying funeral plans for several weeks, remaining hopeful he'd soon return. All three women spoke in detail of the incredible pain they felt in the early days, and how difficult it was to continue with their daily lives. Indeed, Karen and Catherine believe they suffered from depression for a long period of time before seeking professional help. And the lack of understanding and acknowledgment from both family and friends heightened their grief.

Rosenblatt (1996, p. 50) says, for most people, "all that is lost is not realized at one point in time. There is, instead, a sequence, perhaps extending over one's lifetime, of new losses or new realizations of loss." The loss of a future together was a particularly powerful and painful theme repeated many times. "We were supposed to grow old together" was something I heard from each. There was an unspoken expectation that their siblings would be with them forever. This ongoing loss was especially noticeable as family milestones presented. For Karen, the death of her father and the birth of Brian's grandchild brought new layers of sadness. She wished her brother was present to help her through her father's death, knowing that he would have stood with her to present the eulogy. She felt sad imagining how excited Brian would be to have a grandchild. For Rena, her ordination as a rabbi was a key moment she missed sharing with her sister. For Catherine, her daughter's wedding was bittersweet. James and his niece had a special connection, and his absence on such a happy occasion was difficult.

Many of our conversations centered on the relationship that existed while their sibling was alive. Their experiences of grief were directly related to the kind of relationship they shared in life. Each described the unique roles they played for one another and how that role loss carried into their present lives. Brian was Karen's pal and someone who shared her energy and way of operating in the world. She saw him as her one true advocate. Cookie was Rena's dearest connection, a relationship that transitioned from surrogate parent, to best friend, to caregiver. James was like a child to Catherine—something she realized only upon reading the transcripts from our interviews. To understand what was lost, and appreciate the depth of pain, we needed to explore the relationship that was. And through that process of sharing these moments aloud, and delving into the relationship in depth, each felt their stories shift and change, an outcome I will explore in the final chapter.

CHANGED AS A PARENT

> I remember one day my daughter crying, telling me she wanted her old mother back. I guess I was just off the deep end and didn't even know it. I was a walking zombie, probably for at least a year afterwards. (Catherine, July 31, 2008)

> I just remember worrying about myself . . . it was hard because it was a very helpless kind of time for Everett, and it was probably very helpless for the kids, because I was just beside myself. (Karen, June 26, 2008)

Karen and Catherine each had young children when their siblings died. Both spoke of intense grief that overshadowed their ability to parent their own children effectively for a long period of time. Catherine still feels guilty that she was unable to be more present for her daughters during the early months of her grief. She was overcome with sadness and described "walking in a fog." Karen, also, struggled during the first year after Brian died, acknowledging that she remembers very little about how she interacted with her children. "I probably still took them to Brownies," but I don't remember, she said to me. Both women wanted me to interview their now-adult children about their perspectives on this time. They even used very similar words to describe what they thought their children would say. "Ask them . . . they'll tell you I was crazy."

And they acknowledged that after making it through those very dark days, their brothers' deaths changed them as parents.

Buckle and Fleming's (2011) qualitative study of bereaved parents offers an interesting lens on the above. They interviewed 10 bereaved parents about their experiences "parenting" their surviving children. Their data revealed a phenomenon they named "bereaved parenting"—living the experience of parenting while being continuously bereaved. "For a parent, one of the startling and unsettling observations was that the demands of parenting and the demands of grieving collided virtually from the moment of the child's death" (p. 114). Parents were completely overwhelmed by their grief and struggled with the day-to-day challenges of caring for their surviving children. For some, friends and family stepped in to assume the role for a long period of time. All acknowledged that they "parented at a reduced level" (p. 119) for an extended period of time.

The connection between the experiences of bereaved parents and bereaved adult siblings is striking and speaks to the depth and impact of this loss. As mentioned previously, the death of a child is viewed by most as the worst loss and yet, some of the same challenges bereaved parents face, intersect with that of bereaved adult siblings.

After reconnecting with their role as parents, they were changed. Catherine wanted her daughters to understand and value their special connection as siblings. "I tell them, you know, you only have each other. And you need to know that blood is thicker than anything else, and no matter what happens in your life that you two will always be there for each other. You need to be there for each other, because friends will come and go" (Catherine, August 13, 2008). Karen expressed similar sentiments, encouraging her daughters to be present and help one another. Rena was especially upset when she'd hear her children arguing, something that Karen and Catherine also expressed. All agreed that helping their children understand and appreciate their brothers and sisters on a deeper level became central in their parenting.

PROTECT MY PARENTS

I would kind of tread lightly because I was afraid of, of upsetting her. That if I would bring it up or I would say something that she would be upset. On the other hand, sometimes, I wanted us to just be able to talk about her, oh remember when Cookie said this or remember when Cookie did this. (Rena, June 11, 2008)

> The funeral place where we held his service . . . had a tree planting for everybody that had passed away in that year and invited us. My mom didn't want to go. She couldn't deal with it. So we never went. (Catherine, August 13, 2008)

> Here's a cassette tape of the funeral. And you know what's funny? It's that my mom keeps asking for it and I keep saying no. I won't give it to her. . . . I just don't want her to be playing it over and over . . . it's almost like I think I'm protecting her, but who am I to think that? (Karen, June 26, 2008)

"I don't want my parents to feel worse" is a statement I've heard many times from bereaved siblings. When an adult brother or sister dies, the parent and child role seems to flip, almost overnight, and surviving adult children want to protect their parents from further pain. One of the challenges we face as adults is we have the cognitive ability to glimpse the magnitude of the grief our parents are experiencing at the death of their child. And, as many bereaved siblings have children themselves, the realization is even more pronounced. As one said to me, "I don't think I could go on if my daughter died. I don't know how my parents do it." Protecting parents takes different forms. Many try to fill the gap created by the deceased sibling. Perhaps they were the one who called or visited frequently, or the one who helped at family functions, or the one who made everyone laugh. Judy, a bereaved sibling who lost both her sisters in adulthood, described how she moved closer to where her parents lived. "I felt like I had to be there to bring sunshine to my parents' lives. . . . I was the daughter for three" (Marshall, 2012, p. 14). They may try to be a super hero, swooping in to buffer their parents' distress. Others protect their parents through silence. If their parents choose not to speak of their deceased child, the surviving siblings respect the decision and fall silent as well. For all three women in this study, silence was the norm. These two styles of protection are very similar to what Davies (1999) discovered in her work with children. Children often want to alleviate their parents despair and yet, over time, realize that no matter what they do, they cannot—a phenomenon she calls "I am not enough" (p. 198). Buckle and Fleming (2010) also noted their participants (bereaved parents) experienced "almost a role reversal or a blurring of the boundaries between parent and child" (p. 99). Said one parent of her surviving daughter, "She tries to protect us, which means not saying anything" (p. 100). It seems age does not mitigate the pain felt by parents nor the response of children to their parent's pain. They want to fix it.

It's interesting that each are aware of this pattern and yet it is very difficult to break. Whether it's with adults or children though, it is clear that parents play a key role in setting the tone for how families grieve. And for those who face silence, learning to leave deceased siblings out of conversations takes a toll. Not only are they silenced among friends and colleagues who do not validate their loss, but also within their own families, when speaking of their deceased sibling becomes taboo. And, as I will discuss later, being cut off from storytelling, or separated from stories, creates further challenges as siblings attempt to re-establish how to operate in a world without a beloved brother or sister.

CHANGED FAMILY

It's really difficult to get past that bitterness of wanting everybody to grieve the way that you're grieving and interpret—and trying not to interpret it as, well, I'm grieving more than you, I must have loved him more. (Catherine, September 11, 2008)

So that was a huge shift because when the kids got together, there was seven kids and then we went down to four and that was a really big thing. (Karen, July 24, 2008)

So she was really the hub. She was really central to the family. And sometimes that whole matrix that gets rearranged doesn't quite work, and that's exactly what happened in our case. It just didn't quite work. (Rena, July 22, 2008)

I'm often asked if bereaved siblings find solace in discussing their pain with their surviving siblings. And while on the surface it seems a natural avenue for mutual support, in my experience, it is rarely present. Van Riper's (1997) paper about the death of her sister 36 years prior, as seen through the eyes of the surviving five sisters, is a case in point. "Over the years, our family never really talked much about the events surrounding Shelley's death. . . . Maybe it just hurt too much to talk about it. Maybe we didn't want to make each other cry." (p. 587). Our families are not well equipped to deal with such trauma, and so often each member attempts to deal with the pain on their own. Neither Rena or Karen discussed their siblings' deaths with surviving brothers and sisters. As with their parents, the topic simply was off limits.

In addition to the silence, there are often significant shifts in how surviving siblings relate to one another. Relationships with remaining siblings are changed and often strained. Rena was not as close to her older brother and still felt upset that he hadn't made it back in time to say good-bye to Cookie. Catherine, too, struggled with how her brother chose to handle his relationship with James when he was alive. Karen, although not angry with her sister, knew the discord that existed between her brother and sister, making it uncomfortable to talk about Brian with her after his death. The differences in the relationships and the way siblings from the same family dealt with their own grief created tensions. Karen's comment sums it up best: "It's like you end up living the default" (Karen, July 24, 2008). Each woman described their deceased sibling as the one they felt closest to, making it difficult to connect with surviving siblings with whom they did not share that bond. At a presentation (Marshall, 2008) I gave in Montreal, one woman tearfully described how surviving siblings distanced themselves after her sister died. Similar to the awkward comment bereaved parents sometimes receive, "at least you have other children," the presence of other siblings doesn't necessarily ease the pain or provide an automatic avenue for support. I've heard other siblings comment that they make peace with their surviving siblings for the "sake of my parents" and yet the obvious differences in relationships make their interactions difficult. And to Karen's point, siblings attempt to make the best of how their family is left but still long for the one that is missing.

Finally, there is also another change some siblings' experience—the loss of the interplay with their deceased siblings' family. For Karen and Rena there was the additional loss of being cut off from interactions with their nieces and nephews. In Karen's case, her brother's family moved to another province, and they never saw one another again. They spent years celebrating family milestones together and suddenly the entire family was absent. For Rena, she continued contact with adult nieces and nephews for several years but gradually, over time, it faded. Additionally, her niece was uncomfortable talking about Cookie's death, which was another obstacle. For Catherine, James did not have children. The image of a "ghost family" sitting at the dinner table during holiday functions comes to mind. Learning how to be together while missing so many family members is incredibly painful and difficult; and when silence is the norm, it is amplified.

Nadeau's (1998, 2001) work in family meaning making offers some insights into the factors at play. In her study, she conducted interviews with bereaved family members spanning multiple generations within 10 families. She grouped findings into three categories: the strategies by which families made sense of death, a typology of the meanings themselves, and related patterns of family meaning making. "Storytelling was the most common meaning-making strategy. It was used by all families in the study" (Nadeau, 2001, p. 340). She also uncovered "meaning making inhibitors," factors that limited a family's ability to find meaning. "Cut-offs" referred to extended noncontact among family members. Other inhibitors noted were: family rules that limited open sharing, lack of family contact, and absence of family rituals.

Each participant in this study experienced at least one of these inhibitors and, over time, these communication patterns lead to other changes within the families. Karen's family began inviting nonfamily members to events to fill the void created by Brian's missing family. Rena grew more distant from her brother, and visits became fewer and fewer. In Catherine's family, contact was already sporadic and, when they did come together, they never spoke of James. For all of them, the changed family dynamic was another part of the grieving experience they negotiated alone and where silencing was the norm.

SEPARATION FROM STORIES

"We continue to author our own life stories as we reflect, interpret and reinterpret what happens in our lives and we tell and retell our stories to other people and ourselves. Meaning, then is embedded in our life stories" (Gillies & Neimeyer, 2006, p. 38). Telling stories is vital to our well-being. Stories allow us to see experiences differently, build on them, and potentially grow in our understanding of our place in the world. However, for many bereaved siblings, opportunities to share stories about their deceased sibling are rare—first, when we are cut off from talking about them with our peers and then later, when silence becomes the norm in our families.

"Our personal narratives are not merely a way of describing our lives. They are the means by which we bring order" (Gilbert, 2002, p. 224). Sharing grief in community, that is, with others, is the underpinning of many community-based self-help bereavement groups. As previously noted, however, adult siblings are often excluded from these opportunities—specialized groups are not the norm. And, when siblings are also excluded from sharing their pain within their own families, there is a double silencing, removing an important pathway for meaning making.

This insight came to me after a colleague remarked that the participants in this study were not "celebrating" their siblings. He knew someone similarly bereaved who, although deeply saddened by her brother's death, found joy by sharing stories about him with her living brother and other family members. In fact, he remarked, "that's the bulk of what they do when they see one another." I wondered about this for quite a while. "Why were none of us celebrating?" Or perhaps we were and I was missing it due to my own sadness. Then I realized what was different for Rena, Karen, Catherine, and myself. Unlike my colleague's friend who was free to talk openly about a deceased sibling, we were not. We were separated from our stories, first while grieving and later when speaking of our deceased siblings among family became taboo.

"Our stories inform our lives and our lives, in turn, are shaped by our stories. We need to create stories to make order of disorder to find meaning in the meaningless" (Gilbert, 2002, p. 236). Part of recovering meaning is acknowledging that what was lost was meaningful. For many different reasons none of us felt the depths of our grief and sadness were well understood. Later, we missed the opportunity to share happy stories within our families. This was mostly driven by observing the pained reactions of our parents, who we felt needed protection from further sadness. "We make meaning by creating and exploring our stories in concert with other interested parties" (Gilbert, 2002, p. 224). Family members are an obvious first choice but, for participants in this study, that avenue was unavailable.

Siblings are uniquely positioned to be part of stories that extend across entire lives. They know us from birth until potentially well into our eighties and nineties. They see us grow and change and are part of a fabric of experiences that makes life meaningful. I remember my 40th birthday party. Brent would remember it also, for I have photographs of him stuffing some of the designer cupcakes that formed the centerpiece of my table into his mouth. He was present at my 16th birthday party where he played the role of "bouncer." He is in a photograph from my eighth birthday. In it, I am yelling as I reach for his arm, as his hand is plunging into my chocolate cake. It is rare to have a friend present at all of these milestones. Siblings are there first because they are part of the family and later, by choice, when they become friends. When they die, we lose the opportunity to create new stories together. And, when others are uncomfortable remembering stories from earlier days, we cannot celebrate the relationship we had. Our stories end.

I AM DIFFERENT

Definitely more sensitive to people who are grieving and who have had that kind of a loss. (Rena, August 11, 2008)

I think that you become more at peace, but it doesn't . . . it doesn't stop hurting. (Karen, June 26, 2008)

I am probably far more receptive to helping people in need. I have never looked at anybody else on the street the same way as I did before my brother died. (Catherine, October 4, 2008)

"Are you somehow better for having gone through this?" I gently asked Karen. "No," she replied, "for that would be like saying Brian's death was acceptable. . . . I think I've resigned myself [to the fact] that it will never make sense" (Karen, August 8, 2008). When I began this work, Rena, Karen, and Catherine were 10, 7, and 8 years, respectively, removed from their siblings' deaths. I was 18 months. It was difficult to hear their stories and know that the passage of time did not loosen the grip of loss. While the acute pain abated, and they seemed to "get used" to their sibling's absence, the longing remained. They did, however, acknowledge positive changes. Karen described a greater capacity to forgive, no longer holding onto what she now considered minor slights or misunderstandings. When she knew someone needed assistance, she'd pick up the phone and call, proactively seeking ways to assist. When sending bereavement cards, now she included a handwritten note, something she'd appreciated when Brian died. She also consciously encouraged strong family ties among her husband and his brother and sister— reminding them of how lucky they were to have one another. Rena too described moving toward people in need, calling and reaching out, rather than hanging back. She changed her career, gaining additional experience and schooling in pastoral care, now spending her days with patients and families nearing the end of their lives. Recently, she took another step in her educational journey and began doctoral studies in palliative care. Catherine noted she had more compassion for others and also a greater willingness to spend time and share deep feelings with friends and families. She never wanted to walk away from someone and find later that she'd missed an opportunity to be kind. She became more adventurous in life, going after opportunities she might previously have hesitated to chase. And she was much more conscious of and caring toward those living on the street.

Tedeschi and Calhoun's (2008) discussion of posttraumatic growth speaks to me. Bereavement changes most people. For a fortunate few, there is significant growth, almost a breakthrough or transformation to a new level of learning, previously unknown. In many ways, some might say the changes I've made fit this definition. Brent's death led to a new vocation and a deeper sense of purpose in my life. Professionally, I've undertaken roles and responsibilities beyond anything I'd imagined. Creatively, I'm also in a very different place—writing, presenting, and connecting with others in ways I never envisioned. And, on a personal level, my place in his children's lives, as a fully engaged family member in their activities and milestones is an honor I cherish. And yet, I remain permanently etched with sadness at his loss—joy and sorrow sitting side by side (Gibran, 2008).

Within the death education and counseling fields there is a debate about the value of grief counseling and other types of post-bereavement support (Jordan & Neimeyer, 2003; Neimeyer, 2000; Schut, Stroebe, Van den Bout, & Tergehhen, 2001). Some believe most individuals will return to normal levels of functioning without intervention. Now, living the experience of loss, I wonder at what normal functioning is. Perhaps, normal becomes this juxtaposition of deep longing for the life that was, with the knowing that not all the changes are negative. Even as I write those words, I hesitate. Like Karen, I still struggle to acknowledge that anything good can come from such a great loss.

REFERENCES

Buckle, J. L., & Fleming, S. J. (2011). *Parenting after the death of a child: A practitioner's guide*. New York, NY: Routledge.

Davies, B. (1999). *Shadows in the sun: The experiences of sibling bereavement in childhood*. Philadelphia, PA: Brunner/Mazel.

Gibran, K. (2008). *The prophet*. New York, NY: Alfred A. Knopf.

Gilbert, K. (2002). Taking a narrative approach to grief research: Finding meaning in stories. *Death Studies, 26*, 223–239.

Gillies, J., & Neimeyer, R. (2006). Loss, grief, and the search for significance: Toward a model of meaning reconstruction in bereavement. *Journal of Constructivist Psychology, 19*(31), 31–65.

Jordan, J. R., & Neimeyer, R. (2003). Does grief counseling work? *Death Studies, 27*, 765–786.

Marshall, B. J. (2008, April). *Adult sibling loss: Disenfranchised grief and the sibling connection.* Paper presented at annual conference of the Association for Death Education and Counseling, Montreal, QC.

Marshall, B. J. (2012, March). *Adult sibling loss: Stories revised through art.* Paper presented at annual conference of the Association for Death Education and Counseling, Atlanta, GA.

Nadeau, J. (1998). *Families making sense of death.* Thousand Oaks, CA: Sage.

Nadeau, J. (2001). Meaning making in family bereavement: A family systems approach. In M. S. Stroebe, R. O. Hansson, W. Stroebe, & H. Schut (Eds.), *Handbook of bereavement research: Consequences, coping, and care* (pp. 329–348). Washington, DC: American Psychological Association.

Neimeyer, R. (2000). Searching for the meaning of meaning: Grief therapy and the process of reconstruction. *Death Studies, 24*(6), 541–558.

Rosenblatt, P. C. (1996). Grief that does not end. In D. Klass, P. R. Silverman, & S. L. Nickman (Eds.), *Continuing bonds: New understandings of grief* (pp. 45–58). Philadelphia, PA: Taylor & Francis.

Schut, H., Stroebe, M. S., Van den Bout, J., & Tergehhen, M. (2001). The efficacy of bereavement interventions: Determining who benefits. In M. S. Stroebe, R. O. Hansson, W. Stroebe, & H. Schut (Eds.), *Handbook of bereavement research: Consequences, coping and care* (pp. 705–737). Washington, DC: American Psychological Association.

Tedeschi, R., & Calhoun, L. (2008). Beyond the concept of recovery: Growth and the experience of loss. *Death Studies, 32*, 27–39.

Van Riper, M. (1997). Death of a sibling: Five sisters, five stories. *Pediatric Nursing, 23*(6), 587–593.

Research Conversations

Eighty-two-year-old Lillian, in a pink-flowered robe, was dressed up for the occasion. As the nurses wheeled her into her younger sister's room, she started to complain, "Becky, your room is so dark and stuffy. Why don't we go up to my room where it's sunny and there's a better view?"

Rebecca, after more than 70 years of counteracting her bossy older sister's power, smilingly ignored her and greeted the psychologist who had come to the nursing home to interview them about "sibling relationships." The two women were each other's last surviving connection with a large family that had once included their parents and four brothers, all of whom had died.

"Did having a sister make any difference?" the psychologist asked Rebecca. She straightened a trace. Spreading her parchment hands palms up and shrugging quickly, she flashed a glance of irritation to let the interviewer know that he had missed the obvious. "Of course it makes a difference! I know I have a sister! She's my flesh and blood. And I don't even have to see her all the time. To have a brother, to have a sister"—she paused, groping for the right words for her deep feelings. "To know they're just—around—that's all I need to know." (Bank & Khan, 1982, p. 3)

"The view of grief most accepted in this century holds that for successful mourning to take place, the mourner must disengage from the deceased, and let go of the past" (Silverman & Klass, 1996, p. 4). The idea that there is a right and wrong way to grieve is probably one of the reasons many bereaved adult siblings feel they need to stay silent. First, sibling grief is not recognized as being as significant as that of other loved ones. And, second, maintaining a long-term bond with a dead brother or sister is out of step with what society (at least in North America) believes is the "appropriate" way to deal with loss. Everything I have read and observed about sibling relationships

111

(e.g., Bank & Khan, 1982; Cicirelli, 1995; Gill White, 2006; Lamb, 1982) speaks to the strength and importance of such connections. One need only search "sibling loss" on the Internet to find pages filled with living memorials to dead brothers and sisters.[1] And as noted, in my own casual research reviewing the memoriam section of the newspaper, most days there is a message for a sibling long gone. Siblings are permanently etched by the loss of such an intense relationship.

"To experience a continuing bond with the deceased in the present has been thought of as symptomatic of psychological problems" (Silverman & Klass, 1996, p. 4). Most times when I speak about this project with someone from outside the grief community there is an automatic recoiling. And while I understand and recognize the roots of discomfort, I also see how that reaction impacts me. My initial impulse is to go silent. I don't want to add to their discomfort. And yet, I know each interaction is an opportunity to potentially shift a perception. I've learned to push past my own discomfort and talk about how important our siblings are and how devastating their death can be. I see this as another opportunity to change society's script, albeit one person at a time.

Wortman and Silver (2004) suggest that Western society has certain norms or grieving rules that both influence treatment choices and also the level of support individuals feel from others when it comes to grief. One of those norms is that recovery is an endpoint of the bereavement process and that "many still evaluate bereaved people by judging whether they are taking 'too long' to reach this endpoint" (p. 418). There is an assumption that grief will end, individuals will recover and return to their lives unchanged. For bereaved siblings that expectation is amplified. Because their loss is often viewed as relatively insignificant, therefore by design, siblings are expected to "be fine" quickly. And when they aren't, there is genuine surprise. As a neighbor said to me two weeks after my brother's death, "Oh, still sad about your brother?"

---

[1] The following websites and blogs are for deceased siblings. Retrieved May 29, 2009.
http://www.aish.com/spirituality/odysseys/The_Day_My_Brother_Died.asp
http://www.rd4u.org.uk/personal/brother.html
http://tedishere.blogspot.com/
http://www.sibloss.org/memorials/welcome.html
http://www.adultsiblinggrief.com/memorials.htm
http://childsuicide.homestead.com/MemorialSites.html

The idea that grief has an end point, that, somehow, one can cross a line and no longer feel the pain of the loss, is out of step with current thinking that emphasizes a continuation of the relationship. "Memorializing, remembering, knowing the person who has died and allowing them to influence the present" (Silverman & Klass, 1996, p. 17) is more consistent with how bereavement is viewed today. Emphasis is placed on "negotiating and renegotiating the meaning of loss over time" (p. 19). The drive to re-establish meaning or equilibrium after a loss appears to be well entrenched. There is a search for meaning, to understand how our lives are now different because of this loss. Ellis (1993, p. 728), in a personal account of her brother's death in a plane crash, writes, "the sudden loss of my brother threatened, like nothing before, the meaning I had socially constructed for my life, which was that life was by definition meaningful." Her vivid story of first learning about and then managing through the first few days after her brother's death still resonates deeply whenever I re-read it. We expected to live long lives with our brothers and sisters. How could anything make sense when that fundamental truth was proven false?

For Karen, Rena, and Catherine, the ongoing connections they have with their respective siblings were evident in all our conversations. Karen was kinder. Catherine viewed homeless people differently. Rena was able to comfort families as they watched loved ones die. All of these changes came because each one had lost a sibling. It was a way of honoring lives with something positive in their lives lived. And, yet, there was an outside and inside pressure that each of us felt—to move on with our grief. I first noticed it within the context of my work. My boss and co-workers did not understand why, months after Brent died, I continued to struggle professionally. I stopped having lunch with colleagues, saying "good morning," or smiling. I avoided team meetings and after-hour functions. I did not want to be around laughter or engage in what I now considered frivolous conversations about nothing. Both Rena and Catherine shared similar stories of bosses and colleagues who were "out of touch" with what they needed. Catherine recalled her boss saying, "I know just how you feel. I had to euthanize my dog last week."

"A struggle to find significance in the loss is especially acute when deaths are traumatic or 'off time' in the life cycle" (Gillies & Neimeyer, 2006, p. 46). For Rena, Karen, and Catherine, their siblings' deaths were "out of pattern" and "off time." For Rena, Cookie was her closest family member, the one with whom she felt the deepest connection. She took great pride in their close relationship, her joy evident in the photographs contained within her narratives. She looked forward to the many things they would do together in the future. Catherine thought of her younger brother James as akin to her first child, her role as his protector cemented at an early age. His death at the age of 38 ended the possibility that he might finally find his footing and become the "bright star" that Catherine believed he could be. Karen's brother Brian adored her and was likely one of the few people in her life who put her first. She loved the wonderful energy that came from bringing her family together with his and the special connection they shared. Each of these women struggled to rebuild their assumptive worlds (Attig, 2001) in the absence of their siblings. Their early deaths were defining moments around which they needed to reorganize and re-story their lives.

Laverty's (2001) study of bereaved sisters echoes many of the themes noted earlier. Although her work pre-dates mine, I only became aware of it after a chance meeting at a bereavement conference in 2012. I was struck by the similarities both in our personal stories and in what we uncovered in our work. Like me, Laverty, a bereaved sibling herself, chose to explore adult sibling loss for her dissertation. And while our approach was different, there were many intersections that resonate. Laverty's conversations with eight women about their bereavement experiences, and her own reflections on the experience of hearing these stories, are moving. She began each interview/conversation with the question "what has it been like for you to experience the death of your sister/brother" (p. 81) and then let the conversation unfold as the women chose. Using direct quotes from each woman, she articulates eight elements that "collectively constitute this experience as an absence which is a space occupied" (p. iii). Five of those elements are especially similar to sentiments echoed across the narratives in this work. They are: we lived inside each other's pockets, I thought we'd always have each other, the loss is not mine alone, I've changed beyond belief, I will always live with her/him and this loss. While the words may be different, the sentiments express echo the experiences of Rena, Karen, Catherine, and indeed myself in so many ways. And like me, Laverty's position as a bereaved sibling was an asset—with several of her participants commenting that her inside knowledge helped them be more open. They knew she would understand.

Berman's (2009) book, written after the death of her sister, also details similar themes. Siblings recount the changes in their families, their new roles and responsibilities, feeling neglected by others, and the painful realization of a lost future together. Like myself and Laverty (2001), Berman includes direct quotes to illustrate the deeply emotional impact of this loss. She writes: "My sister died. But part of me still cannot believe she is gone. That must be the reason why, years after her death, her name and phone number remain listed on the speed-dial section of my phone. . . . My sister died, and I am still trying to understand and deal with it" (p. x).

Researchers have paid more attention to the impact of sibling loss during childhood and adolescence (Balk, 1990; Davies, 1991; Hogan & DeSantis, 1992; Martinson & Gates Campos, 1991; Packman, Horsely, Davies, & Kramer, 2006; Robinson & Mahon, 1997; Walker, 1993). There is consensus that the loss of a sibling in the early part of life is a tremendously significant event that has far-reaching impacts. When a sibling dies in childhood, parents are left to make huge decisions around the level of detail to communicate to the other children, how to handle the funeral, how to deal with the deceased child's belongings, and so on. It is said that "the surviving sibling becomes a double orphan, losing not only a sister or a brother but also an emotionally available parent" (Bank & Khan, 1982, p. 273). Children are also impacted by how the parents deal with their own grief and what resources are rallied to help them deal with the loss of their sibling. Each participant in this study experienced deep distress over the changes in their family as a result of her sibling's death. Even as adults, their parents' grief, and their own feelings of helplessness to assist, significantly impacted them.

Hogan and Desantis (1996) studied 157 adolescent bereaved siblings and isolated several recurring themes. Siblings had a permanently changed reality of their self and family, recognizing that the death of their brother or sister set their life on completely new paths. They worried about becoming ill and found it difficult to engage in activities for which nonbereaved siblings found fun. There was a strong sense of guilt for feeling happy and, in some cases, for merely living. The "death of a sibling is permanent and irrevocable and shatters all expectations and anticipations of the surviving sibling for a shared future that is not to be" (p. 250). They had difficulty concentrating and ruminated about their sibling's death. Almost all of them expressed a strong desire to reunite with their brother or sister. There was also a strong ongoing attachment to their sibling, demonstrated by continuing to have conversations with their deceased sibling, wearing their clothes, and maintaining artifacts that belonged to them.

We see this same pattern repeated with Rena, Karen, and Catherine. Rena keeps the coffee tin her sister gave her years and years ago on her counter, a visual reminder of their connection through shared cooking. Karen's memory box of Brian is easily retrieved. She likes seeing his handwriting on boxes stored in her garage. It was a reminder of when he helped her pack in preparation for a move and carefully detailed the contents of each box on the outer flap. Catherine keeps James's possessions on display in her home. The photograph he took of his Jeep, a prized possession, is strategically placed on the wall directly in front of her bed. It is the first photograph she sees in the morning.

"Coherence is an achievement, not a given. This is the work of self-narration: to make a life that seems to be falling apart come together again, by retelling and 'restorying' the events of one's life" (Bochner, 1997, p. 429). The acknowledgment that traumatic events and losses have the potential to shatter a person's "assumptive world" (Janoff-Bulman, as cited in Gillies & Neimeyer, 2006), the structures and expectations individuals maintain about the way life will unfold, is not new. And the resulting need to search for meaning after a trauma is well documented in the grief literature (Attig, 2001; Davis, Wortman, Lehman, & Silver, 2000; Fleming & Robinson, 2001; Marwit & Klass, 1996; Michael & Snyder, 2005; Nadeau, 2001; Neimeyer, 2000, 2001; Neimeyer, Baldwin, & Gillies, 2006; Rubin & Malkinson, 2001). Losing a sibling is an "off time" event that shatters expectations for a future together. As Karen so eloquently stated, "It wasn't the natural sequence that things should go, so do I keep on remembering him until the natural sequence isn't there? Will it be okay finally when I'm 90? At least then it will make sense that he is gone" (Karen, June 26, 2008).

Examining this concept against the backdrop of cognitive, trauma, attachment, and constructivist theories, Gillies and Neimeyer (2006, p. 32) proposed three categories of meaning reconstruction: "making sense of the death, finding benefit in the experience and undergoing identity change." Forward and Garlie's (2003) study of bereaved adolescent siblings revealed that the search for new meaning was a core variable in the grieving process. Individual participants described "searching for how this tragedy fit into their life, how it had permanently changed them and how they learned to go on living knowing their sibling was gone forever" (p. 6). Similarly, Batten and Oltjenbruns (1999) suggest a key outcome for bereaved adolescent siblings was a changed world view, one that they created through the process of meaning making.

Like the participants in these studies, Rena, Karen, and Catherine changed old thinking patterns, questioned long-held beliefs, and came to new understandings about the world and their place in it. Karen felt her brother's presence in her heightened intuition. Catherine established a new belief system about death. Rena became more active in her community. All of these changes were part of regaining a set of structures from which to understand life and now death. And their understandings and meaning making continues as they renegotiate the meaning of their sibling's loss in their present lives. "Often the meaning realized by the bereaved are that life is more painful and challenging . . . personal growth often does not mean becoming less distressed, but learning how to become someone who can carry the weight of her or his distress" (Gillies & Neimeyer, 2006, p. 53).

REFERENCES

Attig, T. (2001). Relearning the world: Making and finding meanings. In R. Neimeyer (Ed.), *Meaning reconstruction and the experience of loss* (pp. 33–54). Washington, DC: American Psychological Association.

Balk, D. E. (1990). The self-concepts of bereaved adolescents: Sibling death and its aftermath. *Journal of Adolescent Research, 5*, 112–132.

Bank, S., & Kahn, M. (1982). *The sibling bond.* New York, NY: Basic Books.

Batten, M., & Oltjenbruns, K. A. (1999). Adolescent sibling bereavement as a catalyst for spiritual development: A model for understanding. *Death Studies, 23*, 529–546.

Berman, C. (2009). *When a brother or sister dies: Looking back, moving forward.* Westport, CT: Praeger.

Bochner, A. (1997). It's about time: Narrative and the divided self. *Qualitative Inquiry, 3*(4), 418–438.

Cicirelli, V. (1995). *Sibling relationships across the life span.* New York, NY: Plenum Press.

Cole, A., & Knowles, G. (2001). *Lives in context. The art of life history research.* Walnut Creek, CA: Altamira Press.

Davies, B. (1991). Long-term outcomes of adolescent sibling bereavement. *Journal of Adolescent Research, 6*, 83–96.

Davis, C. G., Wortman C. B., Lehman, D. R., & Silver, R. C. (2000). Searching for meaning in loss: Are clinical assumptions correct. *Death Studies, 24*, 497–540.

Ellis, C. (1993). There are survivors. Telling a story of sudden death. *The Sociological Quarterly, 34*(4), 711–730.

Fleming, S., & Robinson, P. (2001). Grief and cognitive-behavioral therapy: The reconstruction of meaning. In M. S. Stroebe, R. O. Hansson, W. Stroebe, & H. Schut (Eds.), *Handbook of bereavement research: Consequences, coping, and care* (pp. 647–670). Washington, DC: American Psychological Association.

Forward, D. R., & Garlie, N. (2003). Search for new meaning: Adolescent bereavement after the sudden death of a sibling. *Canadian Journal of School Psychology, 18*(½), 23–38.

Gill White, P. (2006). *Sibling grief: Healing after the death of a sister or brother.* New York, NY: iUniverse, Inc.

Gillies, J., & Neimeyer, R. (2006). Loss, grief, and the search for significance: Toward a model of meaning reconstruction in bereavement. *Journal of Constructivist Psychology, 19*(31), 31–65.

Hogan, N., & DeSantis, L. (1992). Adolescent sibling bereavement: An ongoing attachment. *Qualitative Health Research, 2*, 159–177.

Hogan, N., & DeSantis, L. (1996). Basic constructs of a theory of adolescent sibling bereavement. In D. Klass, P. R. Silverman, & S. L. Nickman (Eds.), *Continuing bonds: New understandings of grief* (pp. 235–256). Philadelphia, PA: Taylor & Francis.

Lamb, M. E. (1982). Sibling relationships across the lifespan: An overview and introduction. In M. E. Lamb & B. Sutton-Smith (Eds.), *Sibling relationships: Their nature and significance across the lifespan* (pp. 1–12). Hillsdale, NJ: Lawrence Erlbaum Associates.

Laverty, S. M. (2001). *An interpretive inquiry into women's experience of adult sibling bereavement.* The University of Calgary, Calgary.

Martinson, I., & Gates Campos, R. (1991). Adolescent bereavement: Long-term responses to a sibling's death from cancer. *Journal of Adolescent Research, 6*(1), 54–69.

Marwit, S., & Klass, D. (1996). Grief and the role of the inner representation of the deceased. In D. Klass, P. R. Silverman, & S. L. Nickman (Eds.), *Continuing bonds: New understandings of grief* (pp. 297–310). Philadelphia, PA: Taylor & Francis.

Michael, S. T., & Snyder, C. R. (2005). Getting unstuck: The roles of hope, finding meaning, and rumination in the adjustment to bereavement among college students. *Death Studies, 29*(5), 435–458.

Nadeau, J. (2001). Family reconstruction of meaning. In R. Neimeyer (Ed.), *Meaning reconstruction and the experience of loss* (pp. 95–112). Washington, DC: American Psychological Association.

Neimeyer, R. (2000). Searching for the meaning of meaning: Grief therapy and the process of reconstruction. *Death Studies, 24*(6), 541–558.

Neimeyer, R. (2001). The language of loss: Grief therapy as a process of meaning reconstruction. In R. Neimeyer (Ed.), *Meaning reconstruction and the experience of loss* (pp. 261–292). Washington, DC: American Psychological Association.

Neimeyer, R., Baldwin, S., & Gillies, J. (2006). Continuing bonds and reconstructing meaning: Mitigating complications in bereavement. *Death Studies, 30*, 715–738.

Packman, W., Horsley, H., Davies, B., & Kramer, R. (2006). Sibling bereavement and continuing bonds. *Death Studies, 30*, 817–841.

Robinson, L., & Mahon, M. M. (1997). Sibling bereavement: A concept analysis. *Death Studies, 21*(5), 477–499.

Rubin, S., & Malkinson, R. (2001). Parental response to child loss across the life cycle: Clinical and research perspectives. In M. S. Stroebe, R. O. Hansson, W. Stroebe, & H. Schut (Eds.), *Handbook of bereavement research: Consequences, coping, and care* (pp. 219–240). Washington, DC: American Psychological Association.

Silverman, P. R., & Klass, D. (1996). Introduction: What's the problem? In D. Klass, P. R. Silverman, & S. L. Nickman (Eds.), *Continuing bonds: New understandings of grief* (pp. 3–27). Philadelphia, PA: Taylor & Francis.

Walker, C. (1993). Sibling bereavement and grief responses. *Journal of Paediatric Nursing, 8*(5), 325–334.

Wortman, C. B., & Silver, R. C. (2001). The myths of coping with loss revisited. In M. S. Stroebe, R. O. Hansson, W. Stroebe, & H. Schut (Eds.), *Handbook of bereavement research: Consequences, coping, and care* (pp. 405–430). Washington, DC: American Psychological Association.

Stories and Ripples

Figure 29. "Rebirth."
Source: Family Photo, Brenda, 2008.

When we are aware of the voice of our soul speaking through a story, we feel as never before a connection, a confirmation that we are part of one great interconnected creation. (Atkinson, 1995, p. 47)

I like this photograph. Lying perpendicular is a tree that was once a vibrant part of the forest canopy. Judging by its girth, it lived many years, and then, at some point fell to the forest floor. But that was not the end for this particular tree. Looking closely, one sees incredible growth. Small saplings peer out, larger trees now firmly rooted into its trunk stretch toward the sunlight, and a soothing green moss extends across the length of it. The original tree blends into the surroundings, still present, but now performing a new role in the forest. I took this photograph in 2008 while on a journey to find peace among the great trees of Western Canada. I named it "Rebirth."

One of the unexpected gifts of the original research (Marshall, 2009), was the conversations and new relationships it began. The stories of Rena, Karen, and Catherine became the focal point for presentations and papers. And every time I shared their stories, no matter the medium, someone would write to me. They'd tell me about their deceased sibling and how lonely it was to be an outsider to the circle of support that enveloped others. Sometimes their comments were shocking, like Bill[1], who lost both brothers within a few years of one another. "Friends stopped visiting because they didn't know how to act or what to say." Many told him he needed to live his life carefully as surely his parents would not survive another loss. There was Sarah[2], whose only sister was murdered. Upon returning to work, she faced silence; not a single inquiry about how she was managing. Judy, quoted earlier in this book, who lost both sisters and "lived for three" for the next 30 years. And most recently Carol, a professional in the field, who after her brother's death searched for a sibling group without success. "So here I was, a professional in the field, and I couldn't find a group. And I did not have the energy or the inclination to try to start one on my own." All of these siblings, choosing to share because they connected with one or more parts of Rena, Karen, and Catherine's stories. And the ripples begin.

For every painful and sad story shared, there is most often a glimmer of some change the individual has made or is making, as a result of their loss. In some cases, the change is well beyond a glimmer, and their actions are creating ripples of their own. Ian,

[1] Name changed for this publication.
[2] Name changed for this publication.

whom I met at my very first presentation on this topic (Marshall, 2008), and who subsequently became a bereaved sibling himself, passes copies of the original work to those who he feels might benefit. And if they are open to sharing, he passes their comments back to me, thereby adding to our collective knowledge about this loss. Judy, who also read the original research and wrote to me about her connections to the stories, created a foundation in honor of her two deceased sisters. Each year, near their birthdays, she hosts a fundraiser, "In Celebration of Sisters," thus allowing their stories to continue. Susan, quoted earlier in this text, changed the way her hospice supported bereaved siblings and now actively seeks out the siblings of dying patients to ensure they feel supported. "Sharing stories changes the stories" is something I've said many times. And in the course of completing this book, I came across a new story that has, once again, altered my own.

> Greetings Sweet Sister:
>
> From your oldest brother who is now twenty years old. I passed my birthday quite quietly in the city without knowing it. I quit Nickson's two weeks ago and have been having a fairly good time in town here. The job is finished at Ruby Creek and the stream is wandering through it now. For all one can see it has been in place since the beginning.
>
> Alex McCartney, May 9, 1923

This excerpt is from a letter my great-uncle Alex wrote to his sister Allison (my great-aunt) nearly 100 years ago. At the time he was in Western Canada, one of many stops he made on his travels across North America. He left home in his late teens to look for work and moved across the country by rail, getting off in small towns and taking odd jobs for a few weeks at a time. He communicated frequently with his family, dropping post cards to his mother and long, newsy letters to his sisters from various towns and cities across the country. This one was six pages in length. Alex never returned from his travels. On a cold February night in 1925, he and a friend climbed in a box car that had a small burner operating, generating just enough heat to keep the fruit contained in the car from freezing. Unfortunately, it also gave off an odorless gas, and Alex and his friend were found dead the next day. He was just shy of his 23rd birthday.

This letter is one of about 20 Allison kept until her death some 70 years later. They were in a roll-top desk, neatly bundled together in a small box. As a young adult, I knew of Alex. My grandmother on occasion would mention his name, often get teary, and lament the sadness of his early death. At those times, Allison would fall silent or leave the room. She could not speak of him. Through reading these letters, I learned of the close relationship Allison and Alex shared. Separated in age by only a year, their strong connection came to life for me on these pages. He'd tease her about her advancing age and unmarried status, asking if she was to be a "bachelor girl," and in the same letter, closing with a quick reminder that he was just kidding. In another, he wrote in great detail about the wonderful meals his new farm family was providing, exclaiming "You ought to be here Allie" to enjoy the lemon pudding with real whipped cream. In still another, he enclosed seeds from wild flowers native to the west coast. I could picture my great-aunt, ever the avid gardener, planting those seeds and watching them inch out of the ground that summer. I spent an evening reading through them all, smiling at his comments and picturing the excitement these letters must have generated each time they arrived. And then suddenly, the letters stopped. He was buried in Wyoming, the family unable to arrange transport of his body back to Canada. The local coroner sent a letter with his condolences, a photo of Alex in his coffin, and an accounting of costs. I could feel the dreadfulness that letter must have brought. They'd had their very last conversation.

My great-aunt never married, some saying her brother's death so impacted her, she chose to live a single life. Not long after, her mother took to her bed and by all accounts never left her bedroom. I picture a family rocked by grief, parents mourning their beloved son, and my great-aunt and her sister (my grandmother) mourning their beloved brother. I found only one letter of condolences in the package. It was written to Alex's parents only.

The synchronicity that links our mutual stories is striking and sad. My grandmother and great-aunt lived into their nineties—all those years lived without their brother, whom they so cherished. Reading the letters, feeling the love contained within, connects me to them anew. I asked few questions about Alex when they were alive, reading the timber of the room and knowing that only my grandmother felt comfortable speaking of him. I also didn't understand what losing a sibling meant. I wish now I'd given my grandmother a better opening to share. Perhaps like me, and so many other bereaved siblings, she wanted to celebrate the memories she had of her big brother—the exciting, dapper, and adventurous wanderer. And perhaps like many, she too was surrounded by silence. The power of our stories to change and influence others' experiences continues to amaze me. Just like the ripples formed when a rock drops in a still pool of water, stories are always in motion—shifting, changing, and intersecting in new ways with others. In waves they radiate outward, creating a pattern that sometimes can only be seen from above. This new story, which is in fact a very old one, illustrates that so well.

As I neared completion of this text, I invited Rena, Karen, and Catherine to write readers a letter, sharing whatever they wished. Their stories, as presented in this text, were snapshots from a "moment in time." I wanted to provide a venue to share how their lives continued to evolve and change. We'd been part of one another's journey for several years now, and I knew each of us continued to restory our losses in light of today's experiences. To their words, I now turn.

> This August marked the 15th anniversary of the death of my sister and absolute best friend. In a strange way, it is hard to believe that 15 years have gone by. On the other hand, it all seems so clear as to what was happening that it is like it happened so much more recently. I miss her terribly and have not been able to find a "new best friend" to fill her shoes. Do I want to? No, there will never be another Cookie, who adored me so much and with whom I had so much fun and heartache. But yes, I would like to have a special friend who stands out among the rest. I have friends whose friendship I value immensely, but the friendship I had with her was beyond replacement, I suppose.

> Painful as my loss has been, I have learned about making meaning. This took many years and additional experiences. Since Cookie's death, I also lost both my parents and brother-in-law (her husband), who was like a brother to me. My beloved golden retriever died at the age of only 8 years. As a person who worked in science and clinical research, understanding my grief required a new way of thinking. Answers were no longer based on empirical research. Working on my grief led me to a new path: I decided return to school and embarked upon studies to become a rabbi and upon Ordination, to further pursue training as a chaplain. This is the professional work that I do as a hospital chaplain in the very challenging area of neuroscience,

and I volunteer with Bereaved Families of Ontario facilitating bereavement support groups. I have also begun a PhD in palliative care.

I have learned about the precious and fragile realities of life. I have learned that we are not very different from each other when we are frightened, vulnerable, and grief-stricken. I have learned about kindness especially from strangers, and about how to be kind. Every time I have a special event in my life, positive or negative, I miss my sister. There are times I long to share news with her or to hear her voice, but I have come to know that she has become internalized; she is a part of who I am. My own grief experience has taught me how to support others. She, in her influence and her friendship, has helped to shape who I am and has given me the stamina to do the difficult work that I do; this is a part of her legacy.

Rena

Dear Brenda,

Firstly, I should thank you for all the many hours we spent together talking when you were preparing your thesis. . . . I looked forward to just being able to talk and remember my brother with someone that would listen and not squirm uncomfortably.

Losing my brother will never be "okay," and I will never "be at peace," and I will never "forget." Through our conversations I realized that what I was feeling was okay and people who use those expressions have no idea. Sort of like those books that tell you how to raise children the "right" way. Every day I will see things or hear things that remind me of Brian, and I can celebrate that he is not forgotten.

Two things have happened or been realized in the last few years since your thesis was completed. Probably more, but these stand out.

1) I am not afraid to talk to people about losses they have had because I am worried I will upset them or remind them of their loss. I recently through Facebook spoke to a cousin who lost her sister at a very young age. She said that there were few people that even knew she had a sister and now that her parents have passed away it is as if she never had a sister because no one remembers her. When I sign cards of sympathy it is never

just the "thinking of you" and my name. I feel compelled to write more and share a memory because I know how comforting it can be to know their loved one will be missed. I know that loss doesn't go away or get forgotten and am comforted by people around me that have not forgotten how great my brother was or how important he was to me.

2) Reaching out to my brother's family helps us all heal. It is good for them and good for me. It also is good for our daughters who hopefully will learn the importance of helping people grieve. In the last few years I have been in contact more often with Brian's family that moved to Alberta. My daughter made an interesting point. She said it was easy to think we were hurting more than anyone else because we couldn't see how hard it was for his family so far away. After not seeing Brian's oldest daughter for 11 years, she came for a visit with her husband and two children. What an amazing blessing. It was so great to meet her family and to talk with her. I think seeing each other in person gave us both such comfort. We talked about her dad and how proud he would be of her and her siblings. Her sister had a baby in July this year, and she gave her daughter a female version of Brian's name. This reminds me of how hard it must have been for them and that they think of him as often as I do.

It will never be easy talking with my mom about Brian, and I cannot imagine the loss of a child, but I have also learned to be more understanding that everyone is different and we all deserve the privilege to grieve how we need to. It is not for anyone to judge as to when we should be "better" or "over it."

I know that I will carry the loss of my brother always and will miss him every day. When I hear Neil Young on the radio I know Brian is watching out for me, and those kinds of things I take comfort in. Having friends that recognize my loss and don't squirm quite so much as they used to when I share a memory of my brother has made my journey so much easier. I do not hesitate to share either because I don't want anyone to "feel bad." He was a huge part of me and one of my best friends.

Thanks, Brenda, for helping me figure all these things out. No one wants to have the losses we have had but knowing you were there and "got it" has been such a comfort. Congratulations on your book adventure; so proud to be a part of it with you.

Thanks and appreciation,

Karen

It's been a decade since I lost my beloved brother. When I look back it's almost as if I was in a fog for a couple of years. Things have since improved, but not a day goes by that I don't miss him. In truth, I alternate between anger at him for leaving me, and helplessness that there is nothing I can do to bring him back.

Since my brother's death I have experienced many more losses. What have I learned about grief? Each loss and subsequent grief is unique in its own way. The recent loss of my mom, still so fresh, is again a different kind of grief—a sense of loss so deep, an aching to have even one more hour with her to tell her how much she meant to me.

What have I learned? To live every moment—you never know when it's your last. To tell those I love how much I care about them at every opportunity. Lastly, that life is not to be taken for granted for we never know when our time is up.

Catherine

"Part of finding new meaning was accepting that the pain would be with them forever" (Forward & Garlie, 2003, p. 22). I did not know what to expect when I invited Rena, Karen, and Catherine to write their letters. And while each note positive changes in their lives, the ongoing sadness felt at the loss of their sibling is evident. There is no way to write around this. Some have suggested ending with a positive message would be helpful to readers; human nature is such that we want things to turn out well, for there to be some dramatic shift in thinking that rights the wrong. And yet, as Sullivan (1995) so aptly notes, "Real lives are not like fiction; there can be no comfortable sense of closure, all the loose ends tied, solving the puzzle of a life" (p. 15).

I take comfort in the image of the tree that opens this chapter. It symbolizes what can be. While sadness remains after a sibling dies, and our lives are dramatically altered by their absence, new growth is possible. Our families can reform, tensions easing and new understandings emerging. We can be better at helping others, more empathetic and proactive in our approaches. And our sibling stories can continue and spawn new ones. Hundreds now know of Cookie, Brian, James, and Brent. Alex, my great-uncle whose story might have ended with his siblings' deaths, now also continues. Every time I present, I feel supported by an ever-growing team of brothers and sisters, now departed but very much active participants in our quest. Through them and their living siblings who continue to speak their names, others can glimpse the intensity of this special sibling bond. And once they do, they will perhaps reach out a little differently when they encounter one of us again.

> And when great souls die,
> after a period peace blooms,
> slowly and always irregularly.
> Spaces fill with a kind of
> soothing electric vibration.
> Our senses, restored, never
> to be the same, whisper to us,
> They existed. They existed.
> We can be. Be and be
> better. For they existed.
> (Angelou, 2006, p. 47)

REFERENCES

Angelou, M. (2006). *Celebrations.* New York, NY: Random House.

Atkinson, R. (1995). *The gift of stories: Practical and spiritual applications of autobiography, life stories and personal mythmaking.* Westport, CT: Bergin & Garvey.

Forward, D. R., & Garlie, N. (2003). Search for new meaning: Adolescent bereavement after the sudden death of a sibling. *Canadian Journal of School Psychology, 18*(½), 23–38.

Marshall, B. J. (2008, April). *Adult sibling loss: Disenfranchised grief and the sibling connection.* Paper presented at annual conference of the Association for Death Education and Counseling, Montreal, QC.

Marshall, B. (2009). *Silent grief: Narratives of bereaved adult siblings* (Doctoral dissertation, University of Toronto, Toronto). Available from University of Toronto Research Repository, http://hdl.handle.net/1807/19153

Sullivan, R. (1995). *Shadow maker: The life of Gwendolyn MacEwen.* Toronto, ON: HarperCollins.

Index

About the Author

Dr. Brenda Marshall is a well known speaker, coach, and counsellor from Uxbridge, Ontario, Canada. Her interest in grief work came after the sudden death of her younger brother in 2006. At the time, she was a senior level business consultant at a busy management consultancy. Recognizing the challenges she faced grieving her brother's death while carrying on in her role, she decided to create a resource to support others. The Solacium Group was founded in 2009.

Brenda now splits her time between general organizational consulting through FLOW Learning Group, Solacium consulting, and a busy writing and speaking schedule. She is a sought after expert in the field of Adult Sibling Loss and Grief in the Workplace, speaks at international events across North America and regularly consults with professionals and individuals dealing with loss.

Brenda holds a Ph.D. in Adult Education from the University of Toronto, an M.Ed. in Teaching and Learning from Brock University, a BSc. in Psychology and Criminology from the University of Toronto and has advanced training in Solution Focused and Narrative approaches to coaching and counselling. In addition she is certified in Thanatology: Death, Dying and Bereavement through the Association for Death Education and Counseling® (ADEC).

Brenda welcomes comments, stories and reflections from readers. Please feel free to visit her website: www.solaciumgroup.ca to learn more.